Faith Hope and Injustice

Vin McMullen

ISBN 1901237 23 0

All photographs unless otherwise stated
are from the authors collection

Printed and published by TUPS Books, 30 Lime Street, Newcastle upon Tyne, NE1 2PQ
Tel No: 0191 2330990 Fax No: 0191 2330578

Foreword

Faith, Hope and Injustice is the third instalment of an autobiographical trilogy. To a very large extent it is also a gift that I received from some of the poorest of the poor in several countries in the developing world. It is their story as well as mine — the story of their faith, their hopes and dreams, and their struggle against injustice, which has inspired me. As I reflect on their courage, resourcefulness, sorrows and joys, I am conscious of a deep sense of privilege it is for me to be able to tell their story first hand. It has become something of a cliche that we receive more from the poor than they receive from us, but it is none the less true for all that. This book seeks to give them something back, however small, simply by telling their story as I was asked to do on so many occasions.

While my work and friendship with the poor is the main focus of this book, there are other dimensions, for it is a celebration too of a blessed family life and of the many friendships along the way. While dredging the depths of my memory, all manner of misty pictures and half-remembered anecdotes came to mind. One particular quotation surfaced; somebody once said of somebody else, "He speaks seven languages fluently, but has nothing to say in any of them." Though I have travelled through many countries, I speak only one language, but because of the wit, intelligence and many other gifts of those who hosted me, I believe that I have much to say. This book is a token of gratitude to them for everything — not least for their joy and laughter.

Thanks also to my wife and family. To my wonderful grandchildren; Liam, Ellie, Roisin, Mary, Jordan, Finn and the one just arrived, Joseph James, I say try to remember me as a young man who looked as if he might just be starting to grow old.

Vin McMullen — July 3rd 2001

Gill, this one is for you with all my love.

CONTENTS

Eager Teacher

'For every person who wants to teach there are approximately
thirty who don't want to learn - much'. — W. C. Sellar.

The grey stone building, half-hidden by tall trees and a tangle of vegetation, had a certain charm that crisp autumn morning when I took my first glimpse of St. Aloysius'. At the entrance stood Jack Bourke — a man short of stature, medium build with dark hair greying at the temples, and sallow complexion. He wore his gown with flair looking every inch the headmaster and might even have been taken for the principal of some great centre of learning. He was, in fact, the head of this Secondary Modern Boys' School in the West-end of Newcastle upon Tyne, serving an area with all the social problems of its day. It was 8.30 a.m. and, as yet, there was neither sight nor sound of another living soul. He greeted me with a warm smile and shake of the hand:

'Welcome.... step inside my office. You're the first to arrive, so you may as well sit here for a few minutes.'

Inside, his office was pleasantly untidy with opened and unopened mail, attendance registers, timetables and exercise books covering his desk and spilling on to the floor.

'Light up if you want to.'

I fumbled nervously with my Senior Service while he, looking the picture of confidence and authority, leaned back in his chair, pulled at his pipe producing the sweet aroma of Erinmore, and talked at length about my good fortune at being appointed to this school of great tradition. After some minutes, voices in the corridor and footsteps on the stairs rescued me.

'That's them now.... the staff.... or at least the vanguard of the attack. They'll have the kettle on in a jiffy.'

Jack then fished in his cupboard and produced a cane.

'You'll need this. St. Aloysius' is a tough school, but it's also a good one. Our discipline is firm — very firm.'

And then he sent me upstairs to introduce myself to my new colleagues.

'....And by the way, take the staffroom mythology with a pinch of salt.'

His parting words were almost drowned by a playground that had come to life, as I made my way to the staffroom alone. In an all boys school with an all male staff, it was very much a man's world — rough, ready and raucous, and when I made bold to ease my way through the door, with the hope of not being noticed, I was immediately taken in hand by a grey-haired giant.

'I'm Frank Duffy, the deputy head.'

He pushed me through a thick blue cloud of cigarette smoke and general hubbub and, calling for order several times, announced,

'Could I have your attention please. This young man is our new colleague.... er, what's your name again?.... That's right, Vin.'

'Bloody hell not another Vin.'

'Well, well, well.... now isn't that good to have someone with a bit of class joining us. I have been the voice crying in the wilderness for too long.'

A tiny grey-haired man going bald, with glasses perched on the end of his nose and a cheerful, mischievous twinkle in his eye, came forward to shake my hand.

'Your name spells class, young man — I'm another Vin - Vin Donaghy.'

There followed a succession of anecdotes,

comments and pearls of wisdom, each followed by hearty laughter, which was a kind of welcoming cabaret, as much for their own entertainment as for my benefit. Then Archie Ford stepped forward to introduce himself swishing a cane.

'This is Dotheboys' Hall and I'm Whackford Squeers.'

Photo: Margaret Foster

Canon Wilkinson blessing the shrine in honour of Adam Wakenshaw VC at St. Aloysius' school

Then the staffroom door burst open. It was Jack.

'Gentlemen, it's after nine o' clock and the boys are in their lines.'

There was an abrupt and awkward silence as a group of middle-aged and elderly men slunk out of the staffroom. One of the more mature hazarded a joke to ease the embarrassment.

'It's the new lad, Jack.... leading us all astray.'

In those far-off days, long before OFSTED was invented, St. Aloysius' was an interesting place to cut your teeth as a newly qualified teacher, for there was great support and camaraderie among the staff. The school had a proud reputation for football due mainly to the dedication and skill of Ted Hughes, and everyone boasted of the 'old boy', Jimmy Mullen who went on to play for Wolves and England at outside left.

But its proudest boast concerned Private Wakenshaw who had received the only V.C. to be awarded to any of Newcastle's sons in the 1939-45 War. However, there were few academic achievements — the lads had other aspirations and many were, from an early age, highly competent barrow boys. Parental pressure was virtually non-existent, and as for the teachers, their priority seemed to be to keep order, rather than discipline, thus there were numerous tales told and retold of the exploits of former pupils — their encounters with teachers in school, and with the police force and Durham gaol after school.

One morning a pupil of Vin Donaghy's class arrived late.

'Here boy. Where have you been?'

'Hughes caned me.'

There followed a pupil-teacher encounter culminating in a shriek.

'Who caned you?'

'Hughes.'

Another encounter....another shriek.

'Who caned you?'

'Ow....Oh!...'

'Who caned you?'

'Mr Hughes.'

'That's better. Why did Mr Hughes cane you?'

'For caallin ye Donaghy.'

Incidents like that, both humorous and sad, were commonplace and I learned to wield a cane with the best of them. The efficacy of such practice was never questioned, in spite of the fact that we knew only too well that many of these lads lived with violence at home, met with violence in the streets and when they came to school, yet more of it. Only this time it was in an institutionalised form, for the teachers were children of their time too and lived by the oft repeated maxim, 'Spare the rod and....', which seemed to give it scriptural respectability. After a while I was to question all that, and perhaps conscious of my own turbulent childhood, began to reject the use of corporal punishment, not only for the degrading practice, which it was, but also on the grounds that it simply

Two successful entrepreneurs — St. Aloysius' Old Boys — Albert Sayers (left) Fruiterer, Northumberland Street, Newcastle and Tony Bonner (below) of Oldgate Antiques, Morpeth

did not work, for it was the same boys, day after day, who came back for more — and they were usually from the poorest homes.

It would, however, be a grave injustice were I to make that the last word on St. Aloysius', for it was not a base institution. On the contrary, it was respected and loved by the community it served, for strange as it may now seem, compassion was alive and well among the staff and there really was a good spirit of loyalty and fellowship among pupils and teachers alike — and this in an environment where the teaching and fostering of Christian values was given some priority. There was an ethos which sought to challenge, though it must be said with little effect, the ethics of a sub-culture in which our pupils were immersed. It was thus easy to understand how Jack Bourke could be so proud of his school, *'...... a tough school but a good one.'*

After two years I moved on, and for the next six I gained experience in various schools on Tyneside before being appointed to my first headship, a small Catholic Primary School in Amble in Northumberland.

Amble by name as well as nature, its inhabitants sauntered in the morning, loitered through the afternoon and lingered for the rest of the day — rather like the West of Ireland without a sense of urgency, but they had a rare gift for friendship and hospitality. A small sleepy town standing at the mouth of the River Coquet with a fishing port as its main industry. It also had a lifeboat.

One morning I was met by a dozen or so infants. They crowded around me taking my hand and pulling at my coat while shouting eagerly their exciting news:

> 'Sir, sir, I was up in the middle of the night, on the harbour wall.'

> 'Yes sir, so was I.... it was great.'

> 'Sir, I saw the lifeboat at three o' clock in the morning.'

I could hardly believe what I was hearing. It seemed the whole school had been out of bed for half of the night.

> 'You know, I think you should have been in bed.'

> 'Why sir? The lifeboat was out and they brought fishermen back.'

Then Hannah O'Keefe, my most senior member of staff, pulled me to one side to whisper a word of advice:

> 'Don't criticise.... it's their custom. Everybody who lives by the shore goes on watch when the lifeboat is called out — and that includes the children.'

I looked again into their bright eyes and shining faces and thought,

> 'Of course.... what the hell ....that's exactly where they should have been, celebrating with their mums and dads the saving of lives.'

And the whole school celebrated their good news in Assembly that morning.

Amble was the gateway to the most beautiful Northumberland coastline. The school overlooked the harbour, and in the distance an impressive Norman Castle, dominating the horizon, overlooked the picturesque village of Warkworth, where I took the family to live in an ancient stone house with massive oak beams, damp bulging walls and an old stable to the rear. There, the children romped in the castle grounds and sailed boats on the river, while Gill knitted and I fished for salmon — to very little avail.

It all sounds like Shangri-La, but nothing is perfect — there was little social life and there were no other children in the village. I would have done better to find a house in the more working-class and friendly Amble, but within a couple of years we moved to the small market town of Morpeth where we were welcomed as neighbours by three large families — Devitts, Feeneys and Rutherfords — indeed we were happy now.

Our four children came with me to school in Amble, rattling along twelve miles of country lanes every morning, Rosanne, the bookworm, lost in another world with The Famous Five, John and Andrew chanting, 'Big Geordie, Big Geordie' to the gigantic crane so named, which we passed enroute and which had been recently commissioned for open cast-mining. Rachel endeavoured to raise the tone by singing her full repertoire of hymns, songs and nursery rhymes all the way, ignoring the rude and unappreciative comments of her brothers. The return journeys we made with less haste — in the winter sliding and sledging and sometimes digging ourselves out of several inches of snow, in the spring picking bluebells in woodland and in high summer wading by the seashore. In May 1971 we made a detour for a special visit to Ashington Maternity Hospital where mum had presented us with a new baby, Ben. I can still see their eyes dancing as Gill held their new baby brother to the hospital window for them all to see.

The biggest wrench for us all came in 1973 when I transported my young family two hundred miles, leaving our beloved North-East to take up the headship of St. Edmund's, a large Junior School in Waterloo, Liverpool. But it was all high adventure. On our first visit as a family, the children were dying to hear genuine Scouse spoken, so as soon as we arrived in the big city, I stopped the car to ask a young couple for directions. It could not have been better — or worse depending on your point of view:

'Go up thur and bur left. When you see a chairch tairn right.'

I was suddenly drowned in embarrassment as five mischievous children, who were crowded on the back seat, exploded in laughter. I made a quick get-away *burring left to the chairch on the right.*

When the excitement of my appointment subsided, and I began to contemplate the immense challenge that faced me, that is to assume responsibility for a school with a roll of more than four hundred pupils and a teaching staff of sixteen, I almost fell apart with fear and trepidation. Of course, I did not know then that I need not have worried, for when the time came, I was given the warmest of welcomes by the friendliest and most professionally competent staff I could have hoped for. The parents and children too were wonderful, and the following nine years were to be the happiest of my professional career.

During the final weeks in Morpeth, as I contemplated emptying the home that we loved so well and saying goodbye to so many friends and relations, my mind was in turmoil, for I knew that my heart would remain in Northumberland. I decided therefore to leave a base to which we could return.

West Shield Hill

'There was a time when meadow, grove, and stream,
The earth, and every common sight,
To me did seem
Apparelled in celestial light,
The glory and the freshness of a dream.' — William Wordsworth

It was a motionless June evening, the fields and hedges were fresh and lustrous, so too were the oaks and beeches, bathed in sunlight and heavy in leaf, as I made my way to West Shield Hill Farm for the very first time. It had been something of a scorcher that day, and it was still warm just after milking. Overhead, swallows swooped and dived while the cows returned to their meadow and Bramble, the black labrador, barked her greeting as she ran towards me, and then snuffled around my legs to distract me momentarily from the purpose of my visit. Jim Miller, his wife, Frances, and their three daughters were all out of doors taking the balmy evening air. A look of, 'I wonder what this fellow wants', seemed to be written all over Jim's face. I had come straight from school and felt decidedly overdressed in suit and tie, but was soon put at ease with welcoming smiles.

'Hello', I said, 'I wonder if you can help me?'

'Well now, that depends. What is it you're after?'

'I've got a static caravan and I'm looking for a site.'

'You mean to live in permanently - or just now and again?'

'Let me explain. I live in Morpeth but I'm about to move out of the area - Liverpool as a matter of fact - but my roots are here in Northumberland and I know that I'll want to come back regularly, so the ideal would be to have a base where I could bring the family during school holidays.

I'm not looking for facilities - just a corner of a field out of your way.'

Jim Miller, I was soon to learn, was of a quiet disposition, reserved and pensive. With a stroke of the chin he fell into a thoughtful silence, and standing stock still he gazed into the far distance.

After a while he lit his pipe, spread his elbows on the stone wall overlooking the meadow, and rubbed his chin once more. It was just as well, for it gave me time to utter a silent prayer, for this place looked good and I so much wanted a positive response. It also gave me the opportunity to exchange a few words with Frances and the children; ten-year-old Helen, seven-year-old Janet and three year old Claire, who were playing bat and ball in front of the farmhouse. Eventually, Jim turned in my direction, and a faint smile creased his cheeks.

'What about the stack yard, would that do?'

'Oh, aye', I said, without having a clue what a stack yard might be.'

'Come wi me', he said; 'See what you think.'

Behind stone buildings and well out of sight of the road stood two barns and a byre and an open space enclosed with hawthorn hedge. It looked ideal.

'You could put it there if you like.'

He was pointing to a hollow in the far corner beside an ash tree in tiny leaf. It was an answer to prayer, and I could hardly believe my luck.

Heaven knows what he must have thought when I turned up for the first time with five children - ages ranging from eleven to two — but we soon became friends, and the children from both families romped happily together, picnicking in the meadows, producing plays for the entertainment of their parents in the open, or sometimes in the granary, when the North-East climate played true to form. We walked over stubble at harvest time to the whirr of the combine harvester while rabbits jumped and kicked and fled, and in the evening we all worked together under Jim's direction with the adventurous task of building a straw stack next to our caravan. On one truly memorable occasion I even helped to muck out the byre, and afterwards, was glad to be hosed down by Gill before being allowed inside. We also, from time to time, swam in the local swimming pool and, further afield, walked on the Simonside hills. Happy days always seem more radiant when viewed in retrospect, and those children, some of them now parents themselves, remember them as the golden years of childhood - as for me they will always remain the blessed years of parenthood.

Thus West Shield Hill became much more to us than we had ever intended it to be. Initially, it was to be merely a bolt hole where we could spend a couple of days, from time to time, while visiting my mother, relations and friends, but soon it became our resort to fly to during summer holidays and a place of happy memories to excite our imagination during the dark days of winter. It was my hide for birdwatching too, for sited in

West Shield Hill Farm — more than a bolt hole — a second home

very close proximity to the hedgerow and within a few yards of a copse, I spent many happy hours watching wrens and robins, blue-tits and yellow-hammers building, pecking and preening. One morning a deer, unaware of my presence, jumped a fence and nonchalantly sauntered past the kitchen window. How many times have I sat under the ash tree dreaming dreams and contemplating a kestrel hovering overhead, while taking in the odours of hay, crisp and sweet in high summer, and giving a wave to Jim as he chugged past in his tractor. And how many times too have I sat there at night, untroubled by the pollution of street lighting, captivated by the night sky and spellbound by a million stars. In truth, it had become a kind of second home.

The years were passing too quickly - so too was middle age, and the hankering for world travel receding, for the opportunity had passed me by, or so I thought. But 'times they were a-changing', and almost without warning early retirement became an option and I seized the opportunity.

Golden years of childhood

Rachel, Ben and Gill feasting on the splendour that is Northumberland

Holy Ground

*'The Lord called to him from the burning
bush and said, " Moses! Moses!"
He answered, " Yes, here I am."
God said, " Do not come any closer.
Take off your sandals, because you
are standing on holy ground."' — Exodus C3 v4-5*

'What the hell am I doing here?'

I must have asked myself the same question at least a dozen times as I lay awake during the long night in the pitch blackness of a Manila slum.

A few hours earlier, Sister Evelyn of the Good Shepherd Congregation had guided me through Manila's noisy and congested city centre and along backstreets, where hundreds of families, slum-dwellers, lived on wasteland, under rubbish, in a world of unbelievable squalor and degradation. Surprisingly, their neighbourhood was lit-up. A tangle of overhead cables carried stolen electricity from street lamp posts in the metropolis, and a group of young men, attempting a version of basketball under floodlights in this most unlikely setting, stopped their game so that they could stand and stare. My arrival on the scene had caused something of a stir. Every head turned in my direction, and children running from the dark alleys to the right and to the left shouted their greeting:

'Hi Joe! Americano?'

They encircled me, some leading the way, some walking alongside, and others following close at my heels, as they ushered me noisily into their locality. Eventually we stopped outside a low structure, one of a long line of terrace shanties, composed of cardboard, plywood, plastic and bits of tin. Inside, an oil lamp burned and I could see a couple on their hands and knees cleaning the

Living among rubbish

plywood floor with damp rags. Sister Evelyn took my elbow and ushered me inside.

'Vin, meet Connie and Brecky.'

Connie and Brecky were to be my hosts and I was to share their home for the next twenty-four hours. After brief introductions, Sister Evelyn returned to her convent. Thus, I was left alone with a mother, father and four sons who spoke practically no English, in a space measuring seven feet square, with neither a cushion nor a stick of furniture to relieve my physical discomfort, and a deep sense of foreboding that this was to be a long night.

As we attempted to communicate in sign language and the odd spoken word, neighbours started to arrive. Leaving their plastic sandals at the entrance, they sat barefoot and cross-legged on the plywood floor. The tiny dwelling was packed beyond belief, and for the next few hours, there was a constant coming and going amidst a babble of conversation in which I could take little part. The children squeezed their heads through the doorway and fixed their gaze on me as if they expected that at some moment I might levitate, or even explode. Then a bright-eyed, middle-aged man with a goatee beard and dressed in denims appeared on the scene. Holding out his hand and speaking in good English he said,

'Hello, my name is Ding. Are you American?'

'No, I come from England.'

'I have been to England - to Liverpool. I know Pierhead and two Cathedrals.'

I could hardly believe what I was hearing. Here, at the other end of the world, in the back of beyond, living in a Manila slum, was a man who spoke good English and who was familiar with places very close to where I lived.

'I was seaman. I go to many countries. I like England. Why you come here?'

I explained as best I could that I was employed by CAFOD, an agency of the Church in England, which sought to work in partnership with the poor in the developing world, and that I had come to learn at first hand from the people themselves. My purpose was to gain a better understanding of their problems and how they were facing up to them. He passed on that message to those who sat motionless on the hard floor, while I shuffled uneasily on aching buttocks. The questions and answers that followed were a two-way process and seemed to go on forever. In truth, they showed as much interest in me, my family, home and country, as I did in them. Then Connie produced a bible, well-thumbed and soiled. Someone read a passage and an animated discussion followed. Ding, sitting close-by, and solicitous for my welfare, whispered a translation into my ear. They sang a hymn, said a prayer and then thankfully sat in silence. My own silent prayer was that they would call it a day, for I was sore, itchy from mosquito bites and desperate to lie down full-stretch. Eventually the visitors all drifted back to their own dwellings, and my hosts indicated that, as guest of honour, I should sleep on what appeared to be a piece of brightly coloured curtain material.

But it was by no means the end of the day for Connie.

'I sell baluts.'

I looked puzzled and then she produced a small basket containing eggs. I was given to understand that there was something different, even special, about these eggs, but quite what it was, no amount of word-searching or sign language could convey, until Brecky took one into his hands, broke the shell to reveal a fully formed chick, and with great aplomb, popped it into his mouth and devoured it. My look of astonishment communicated my thoughts graphically, which caused the children's eyes to light up in spite of their tiredness, and they laughed heartily. Brecky merely smacked his lips to emphasise the point that baluts were a delicacy.

I later learned that baluts were indeed a delicacy in the Philippines, and Connie every day purchased fertilised eggs that were almost ready to hatch. She then boiled them, and in the evening, she took herself and her baluts to the red light district of Manila, where she sold them in the streets in order to earn a few pesos to buy rice to feed her boys.

Before retiring, I slipped outside to explore the toilet arrangements. As I feared, they turned out to be a public affair, at least for the menfolk, so I returned to my cotton sheet and plywood mattress in great discomfort.

Back inside, the atmosphere was hot and sticky, and my bladder fit to burst. I tossed and turned and scratched while those around me snored and coughed. Sometime later all became quiet outside. I took to my feet and banged my head against the low, corrugated tin roof. The baby cried and the anxious mother stirred. I crept through the hole in the wall, which served as entrance and exit and for a few blissful moments I stood under the stars and enjoyed the feeling of being quite alone - even among a sea of mud and garbage. Privacy, I had come to understand, is a luxury hardly known to the poor. With no inhibitions now, I relieved myself on the edge of the litter-strewn pathway as both custom and necessity dictated, and where a few hours earlier, young people had gathered to socialise and flirt, while their parents gossiped and tiny tots with large sleepy eyes had stared lethargically at one another while clinging to their mothers' skirts. Malnutrition was everywhere.

Eventually, I crawled back inside, in the hope, though not the expectation, of snatching a few hours sleep. Though the night was still young, cocks in nearby shanties started crowing.

'What the hell am I doing here?'

I repeated once more,

'sleeping under garbage, being eaten alive and dying of thirst, when I could be enjoying home comforts in the bosom of my family?'

It was called an Exposure Programme that brought me to the Developing World - its purpose, they said, was to give me a better understanding of the problems of Third World Poverty in general, and specifically, to share the daily experience of the poorest of the poor in The Philippines. It was a baptism of fire.

I lay awake in pitch blackness entertaining a jumble of emotions and thoughts, for though it seemed like light years away, I reminded myself that it was just 48 hours since I had lived in another world enjoying domestic bliss. I compared and contrasted those two worlds. In England it was tea-time, and my home, which now in my mind's eye had taken on the proportions and opulence of a palace, would be echoing to noise of footsteps on the stairs and the chatter and banter of my two youngest, Rachel and Ben, in from school:

'What's for tea, Mum? I'm starving.'

I reflected how none of us had ever experienced hunger - appetite yes, but never real hunger - and now as I lay there I became deeply conscious that I was surrounded by families who go to bed hungry every night.

John and Andrew would be arriving now from their day's work and, as usual, they would treat the neighbours to a feast of pop music at full volume, while Gill, their mother, would start busying herself in the kitchen preparing another feast, of the belly kind, with every modern convenience and access to clean water at arm's length. Rachel would surely be taking a shower, for that was her unalterable routine. I thought too of Rosanne, our eldest, now living away from home, embarking on a professional career as a newly qualified teacher and full of hopes and dreams.

Here I was living with another family with no hopes and no dreams living in a dwelling of unbelievable deprivation no bigger than our bathroom, and the children, though clearly malnourished, never announced that they were starving, nor did they ask,

'What's for tea?'

They knew it would be rice. It was always rice. On the odd occasion, Brecky might be fortunate enough to catch a fish from the heavily polluted waters of Manila Bay. But that was a rare event. The young people had no record players - they had nothing! And those neighbours who had come to visit me, leaving their plastic sandals at the doorway, they too had nothing. This was truly a community of the poorest of the poor, who collectively owned less than what I carried in my back pack. The cost of my camera alone would have fed the whole community for a month.

I reflected too on their faith. Clearly, these people lived in the presence of their Lord, and in my mind's eye I once again saw that pathetic heap of footwear, and realised that I too should have removed my shoes as I entered - not merely to leave the filth outside, but as has been said before, because I was on holy ground - God had been there before me.

"They knew it would be rice — It was always rice."

A gentleness and cheerful curtesy that I did not expect from people living in such appalling conditions

Land of Smiles

'Happy are you poor; the Kingdom of God is yours!'
Luke C6- v20

"So happy they don't know how miserable they are"

It was five o-clock in the morning when, through the cardboard wall, I heard the sound of voices and the clinking of buckets which heralded the new day. Then I heard the family stirring, though in the darkness I could see nothing. It felt like midnight as I crawled outside quite unprepared for the shock that was to come - the bright sunlight pierced my eyes and struck me blind for a full minute. Then I took in the remarkable scene. There were children everywhere, each with a bucket filled to overflowing. There was a dunking and dousing, a rinsing and wringing, of white shirts and grey shorts accompanied by a liberal spilling of soap suds. Then clothes lines were strung across the crowded alley-way and school uniforms were hung up to dry. The water was not discarded but put to good use - they poured it over their heads, and then with squeals of delight, they proceeded to scrub themselves, and each other, in a festival of mirth and hygiene.

When they became aware of my presence their capers became even more animated - playing to the gallery! I was a good audience and laughed with them. Each in turn called,

'Hi Joe,'

but, in my unwillingness to accept a change of name and nationality, I responded,

'Good morning. I'm Vin from England.'

They giggled, and then dozens of voices began shouting and repeating,

'Good morning.... Good morning.... Good morning Vin from England.'

And then they giggled all the more at their own virtuosity.

Mothers, with babes in arms, and fathers, while keeping their distance, caught my eye and beamed a welcoming smile. Even the dogs, the skinniest in the whole of creation, barked their greeting as

'Dunking and dousing, rinsing and wringing'

they scuttled around my feet, while roosters continued their raucous calls from hidden perches. The whole atmosphere oozed happiness and, in spite of my sleepless night, the discomfiture of thirst and mosquito bites, a strange feeling of, *'It's good to be here'* entered my soul and I smiled and laughed with everyone.

Connie brought a bowl of boiled rice and Ding arrived carrying a teapot and two mugs. He settled himself on a heap of old car tyres and invited me to join him.

'The water has boiled, so the tea is safe for you to drink.'

He handed me a heavily stained tin mug, into which he poured tea that tasted as if it had been sweetened with a mountain of sugar but, in spite of that, never was a drink more welcome.

'I have something to tell you.'

Ding had the self-satisfied smile of one who was about to impart news of some importance.

'Mrs. Thatcher and her Government have been bombed.'

'What?'

I tried to say more, but I was lost for words as I stared vacantly into his laughing eyes. Was this some sort of joke? He paused for a while as if to tease, and then his smile broadened as he enjoyed my astonished reaction.

'Yes, their hotel bombed by I.R.A. Some killed, some injured, but Mrs. Thatcher no injury. I hear it on radio - very big news!'

I confess to a mixture of thoughts and emotions, as I considered the various reactions to this news back home, and I was desperate to know more, but that was all he could tell me, for the story had just broken on World News. I was thus left to reflect, that on the one hand, everything that I was experiencing here - climate, language, culture, to say nothing of the living conditions - told me that I was in another world, and yet, out of the blue comes a reminder that we all live in a global village.

'In Philippines we have conflict too. Here the N.P.A. (New Peoples Army) are the leaders in our struggle for social justice and oppose the Marcos Dictatorship. There is no freedom to oppose politically, so N.P.A. oppose militarily.'

I sensed that Ding had an agenda. That there was more information he wished to impart was obvious, but his concern was not about the British Government, however dire their present state of affairs, but rather about the Philippines' situation, which was after all what he presumed to be the whole purpose of my visit. But just then a major distraction diverted my attention. Children in their droves started to emerge from nowhere and formed themselves into a jabbering and joyful procession, some barefoot, others in plastic sandals, but all of them spotless in white shirts and grey shorts and carrying school bags over their shoulders. Their whole appearance would have been acceptable, without question, in any middle-class Primary School in Britain. As they passed by, they flashed a thousand smiles in my direction and some shouted over and over again,

'Hi Joe! Good morning.... Good morning Vin from England.'

They took with them their exuberance and noisy chatter, and their departure brought about a change of tone, and a strange tranquillity descended upon the neighbourhood.

But now it was their mothers' turn to capture my attention, for standing barefoot by their own doorways, and wearing cotton dresses, they poured water over their heads and soaped and rinsed themselves. They then withdrew into their dark caverns to reappear minutes later sparkling and wearing a change of dress. Their jet-black hair, combed back, glistened in the morning sun, and though tiny, these young mothers with head erect stood tall and proud. I reflected that anyone meeting them out of their context, on any of the main thoroughfares in town, would never guess that they had emerged from the most appalling living conditions imaginable.

Sister Evelyn appeared on the scene, to take me on a walkabout through narrow alley-ways and a maze of shanties, where I was to absorb other images that would remain vivid in my memory for the rest of my life.

> 'Watch where you put your feet. As you will have discovered, there's no sanitation here, and that's an open drain.'

She pointed to a foul-smelling shallow ditch, which ran alongside a row of shacks. Here and there, small children played among the dust and filth, and grandmothers no doubt, looking much older than their years, sat on boxes and upturned oil drums, smiling, and waving a greeting to us, while their menfolk, standing idly in huddles, sucked at home-made cigarettes, coughing and spitting into the grey, stinking waters of the open sewer.

As we continued, we exchanged smiles and touched the heads of babes and toddlers until, in sudden contrast, we hit upon a sombre group of women speaking in hushed tones, in the centre of which a young mother, red-eyed and with tear-stained cheeks, was being comforted. On seeing us, she fell upon Sister Evelyn and sobbed. Though not a word could I understand, somehow the language of a broken heart told me that this poor woman had lost her child. I was in something of a daze with fatigue, the blistering heat of the mid-morning sun and dehydration, but through

'And Grandma had a shower too'

the mist, I felt a hand on my elbow and heard a voice.

> 'It happened last night. Her baby boy - just six months old. We must go inside to pay our respects. It is the custom.'

On a wooden trestle stood a white cardboard box and inside, like a wax doll, lay her beautiful baby. I was struck dumb for several minutes, then Sister

Evelyn, sensing that I was more than a little overcome, whisked me away.

'Let's go to the convent. Sisters Clare and Catherine are expecting us.'

The notion of a convent conjured in my mind the familiar picture of a large house sparkling in a dust-free zone of some leafy suburb with polished floor, fine furniture and furnishings and smelling of wax polish and incense. I guessed that the convent to which I was heading would be somewhat different. I was not disappointed. Situated close to the hovels of the poor, it was a small bamboo house divided into three — chapel, dormitory and living room-cum-kitchen. The Sisters were waiting to greet me with smiles and a most attractive if simple breakfast table. I wallowed in the luxury of sitting on a chair and slaking my thirst with ice-cold water from their fridge. When a boiled egg was placed before me, my disquiet must have been obvious, for the three Filipinos paused and looked concerned.

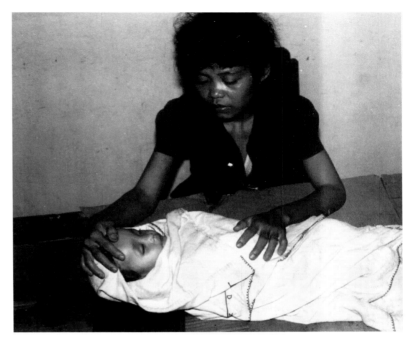

Mother with her dead child

'Is this a balut?' I asked.
The Sisters collapsed in an explosion of laughter.

'How do you know about baluts?'

I gave a graphic account of Brecky's demonstration and, once again, they laughed heartily.

'You are learning about the Philippines very quickly. But let me assure you that our hen laid that egg especially for you —just one hour ago.'

While I ate, the conversation - a mixture of small talk and pleasantries - continued, but somehow I sensed that the nuns too had an agenda and were about to create an opening.

'You were very upset by the death of the baby?'

I pondered for a while, picturing that little white cardboard coffin within two metres of an open sewer, and then continued in silence for a little longer with other thoughts.... then, wanting to make some connection with home, I suggested,

'Of course, children die in my country too, and the sufferings of their mothers, rich or poor, are the same the world over.'

My thoughts had once again transported me back to my own family situation, and I remembered only too well when in the early years of married life, the stillbirth of our first-born shattered our lives — bringing disappointment and deep sorrow when all we were expecting was joy and happiness. The young sorrowing mother that morning had reminded me too of the heartbreak of Gill, who despite the fact that she has since reared five healthy children, still visits the grave of *our little Clare*, and sheds a tear. But those thoughts I kept to myself and so my comment might well have been misunderstood and may have appeared somewhat insensitive in the Philippines context, where infant funerals are almost a daily event. In rather a clumsy way I added,

'Of course, infant deaths are rare in a rich country like Britain, by comparison to a poor country like the Philippines.'

This was her cue and Sister Evelyn seized the opportunity. It was obvious, by her instant reaction, that I had pressed the right button, for she became animated, her eyes lit up and her hands danced, giving emphasis to the rich tones of her Philippines accent.

'No, Vin, the Philippines is a very rich country, rich in natural resources such as rice, fruit, sugar-cane, and we are the world's chief exporter of coconut products. But, more than that, The Philippines is rich in minerals - gold, copper and nickel. This is a rich country, but the masses are poor. Eighty per cent of our people live in absolute poverty. Why? Because our country is being raped by big companies - multinationals, and they are aided and abetted by the rich and powerful of our own people - especially Marcos and his cronies. Our problem is not a lack of resources but a lack of justice.'

The three sisters continued in this vein for some time and I really was interested for several minutes. However, as soon as I was gorged with rice and boiled egg, and my thirst satisfied, the room became a haze, faces and voices kept coming and going, and my chin kept hitting my chest. I fought desperately to be attentive and to appear brisk.....

It was late afternoon when I was awoken to the barking of dogs and the chatter of children. Lying on a mattress in a darkened room, it took some little time for me to become orientated, then I heard the sound of familiar voices. When I stood up, the creaking of bamboo beneath my feet signalled to others that I was awake. A voice called,

'Hello, Vin, are you alive or dead?'

'A little bit of each, I think. How did I get here?'

'You walked, but I think that you were unconscious. All I did was to guide you and take off your sandals.'

Once again I knew that I was on holy ground — but this time I was in the nuns' dormitory!

Solidarity

*'Solidarity is undoubtedly a Christian virtue.... it
is the distinguishing mark of Christ's disciples.'*
Pope John Paul *'Sollicitudo Rei Socialis'.*

I now felt well rested and even sprightly, but an hour or so later I was once again dropping with tiredness. And that is the way it was for three or four days, when I fluctuated between brief periods of briskness and long periods of exhaustion.

Undoubtedly, jet lag had something to do with it - so too had the climate, but the basic error of having taken too much alcohol and too little sleep on the long haul flight of twenty hours from Gatwick to Manila was the biggest single factor, for I was part of a sixteen-member delegation who while in transit spent most of the time socialising and getting to know one another. This accounted for the numerous times, during the early part of the Exposure Programme, that I found myself swaying in a semi-comatose condition, while trying desperately to appear bright and alert.

The rain returned in the evening with a vengeance as I made my way, once again accompanied by Sister Evelyn, through the crowded and noisy metropolis. It was my first experience of a tropical storm, which seemed like heaven's dam had burst, and within seconds the main roads were like rivers.

The older vehicles, unable to cope with the deluge, simply died, causing others to halt and frustrated drivers to hoot incessantly, adding chaos to confusion. Below a forest of umbrellas, pedestrians waded ankle deep, jostling and calling to one another in what might well have been light-hearted banter, but to the stranger in a strange land the babble, accompanied by the blare of the traffic, seemed like mayhem beyond belief.

Then suddenly the rain stopped. We continued our journey, thoroughly soaked and bedraggled, through a sea of smiling faces to a large building which vaguely resembled the stereotypical version of an English convent. There, all the participants of the Exposure Programme were assembled and awaiting our arrival.

We had all been introduced to the Philippines in similar fashion - the focus very much centred on the problems and sufferings of the people, so the next day was given to sharing our experiences. This was a very moving and enriching part of the programme. It was also a time for what our hosts termed *'Orientation'* - social analysis in the context of Gospel values spiced with a pinch of Marxism.

The history of the Philippines we learned, was a history of colonialism - Spanish, American and Japanese. Since the Cold War was still with us at that time, the United States now valued these islands simply for their strategic importance as military bases, while their servicemen denigrated Filipino culture and contributed little to the economy except in creating a degrading sex industry.

Our hosts spoke in slogans too. Big business in the form of *'rapacious multi-national corporations'* was the problem, not the solution. Filipinos had never been able to *'sing their own song'*. But the catchword on everyone's lips was *'solidarity'*. That appealed to me - it was the word that, since my youth, had most captured my imagination, for its meaning seemed to combine the political struggle for justice with the biblical notion of the Kingdom of God. It was exciting to be with people whose politics and faith were one.

In solidarity we were to experience the problems of the poor at close quarters, in a country where more than eighty per cent of the population were living below the poverty line, where thousands of families were dispossessed - rendered landless and homeless by multi-national corporations, where those who opposed or spoke up against injustice were silenced - either by imprisonment or *'disappearance'*. We were to share in the sufferings of the people, stand with the workers on the picket line, meet the families of those imprisoned, and participate in anti-Marcos demonstrations — the *'Parliament of the Streets'*. During this time, my close pal was Joe Ryan, a Dublin man and parish priest in London. Joe was tall, a gentle giant and quietly spoken with a puckish sense of humour. But our close association was not to last, for after a few days, we were subdivided into small groups and I was to visit another island in the archipelago where I was to stay in a Basic Christian Community, listen to the stories of tribal Filipinos, and spend some time with farmers and fisherfolk.

The next morning, with four of my colleagues and two of our hosts, from our partner agency, I flew out to the island of Mindanao in the south of the Philippines archipelago.

Land of Promise

'This we know, the earth does not belong to man,
man belongs to the earth. This we know, all
things are connected, like the blood which
unites one family. All things are connected.
Whatever befalls the earth, befalls the sons
of the earth. Man did not weave the web of life.
He is merely a strand in it. Whatever he does
to the web, he does to himself.' — Chief Seattle

Bhavana, who worked at CAFOD Head Office in London, was Indian by birth, so she took Asia in her stride. Father John had several years' overseas experience, working as a missionary priest in Africa, so it seemed to be no big deal for him either. But for Teresa, Barry and me, this was the thrill of a lifetime.

> 'Welcome to Philippines Airlines. This is your captain speaking. We are preparing for take off, so please fasten your safety belt....'

Minutes later, from a height of 20,000 feet, I was viewing the islands of the Philippines. It was difficult to take in, that after several months of preparation, all this really was happening to me, and a window seat seemed to be the very pinnacle of privilege as I picked out tiny fishing vessels in the South China Sea and struggled, with the help of a map, to give a name to each of the islands below. For some time I became spellbound by the splendour of it all. The sun shone brilliantly, illuminating each snow white cotton wool cloud, and the sky and sea were of the deepest blue. From this perspective, the whole world seemed to be bright, clean, and colourful — light years away from the filth and stench of the slums of Manila, and my camera clicked with ridiculous optimism.

But in spite of my elation, or perhaps because of it, I was moved to reflect on how far I had travelled, not merely on this trip, but on life's journey, for other times came to mind, when in similar fashion, I had tingled with excitement at the thrill of the moment. I drifted into a state of deep nostalgia, recalling the day, many years ago, when I stood on Cooper's Hill overlooking Runnymede, basking in the aura of privilege, impressive buildings, extensive lawns and landscaped woodland which surrounded me and realising that all this was mine for a little while - for I had made it to Teachers' Training College. The miracle of sitting in an armchair, travelling at several hundred miles an hour at a height of 20,000 feet, faded from my consciousness as I became absorbed in happy memories of student days when we worked hard and played even harder, swimming in the Thames, dancing on the lawns in high summer and drinking gallons of beer in the Barley Mow at Englefield Green.

Among the student body, there was a spirit of euphoric camaraderie — everyone blessed with a hundred friends — and I boasted of having John Mortimore as room mate, though in truth, I shared him with more than a dozen others in dormitory accommodation. I do claim, however, to be one of a favoured few who spent many a Saturday afternoon among the elite in the stand at Stamford Bridge - for John was Chelsea's centre-half. That too was a thrill!

Peter Toole was another who had distinguished himself. He was a member of the English folk dance team and was widely travelled - not only to Folk Festivals around Britain and Europe, but also in Asia, where he had served in the Army during his National Service. His tales of trekking through the Malayan jungle, wading through rivers in full kit, being sucked by leeches and bitten by mosquitoes in the war against terrorists, kept us awake until the wee small hours, for Peter was my closest pal and another of my room mates.

'I'd love to travel the world one day, but not as soldier. There was a time when I wanted to be a missionary priest, but not now - and yet I'd like to do something with a sense of vocation - perhaps teaching and working with the people in the Third World is what I'm hankering after.'

Peter was a fervent Christian - an Anglican - so to a very large extent we spoke the same language and he understood what I meant by 'sense of vocation', but these were the days of heated debate among Christians, before 'ecumenicism' had been invented, and we burned the midnight oil discussing such things as the English Reformation, the Eucharist and Papal Infallibility - no doubt boring our more normal pals, who spent their energies chasing the lasses from Royal Holloway College, just down the road.

Then there was Jim Cavanagh, a mature student and widower, who had suffered the loss of both wife and baby. It was early in the second term that we noticed a spring in Jim's step as he whistled through the college grounds. There was a twinkle in his eye too and we all teased him unmercifully until one evening, over a pint, he spilled the beans - he was head over heels with a young lass from North Finchley, whom he had met while working as a temporary postman during the Christmas holidays. As the weeks and months passed, his love affair blossomed and Jim spent many hours thumbing lifts to Durham where his girl friend, Zillah, was a student at the university. He often spoke of Zillah's younger sister, Gill, who was a student teacher at St. Mary's Training College in Newcastle.

'When you're home on holiday, give her a ring. She's a nice girl.'

But I was very definitely having none of that .... until, that is, at closing time one evening when I, and half a dozen pals, fortified by Newcastle Brown Ale and oozing dutch courage, piled into a phone box on Wallsend High Street to serenade Gill Burgess with a choral rendition of 'True Love'. It must have sounded exquisite! I followed up with a clumsy request for a blind date.

'How could I possibly agree to my seeing you when I don't even know you?'

'Well, I don't know you either, but I'm willing to take a chance.'

She must have been desperate. Or perhaps it was just my cheek that pulled it off? The next evening we strolled hand in hand through the streets of Newcastle, drank coffee and smoked cigarettes in a cheap cafe. Then, penniless, we kissed goodnight and clinched under the stars, and not even the stony gaze of the Sacred Heart statue in the college grounds at Fenham could cool my ardour - and that was another thrill!

But the biggest thrill of all was when, in St. Alban's, North Finchley, in a church packed with friends and relations we were wed. Cousin Jim, now Father Cuthbert, did the honours. We walked to our reception, across the road, in St. Michael's Convent, Gill's old school, and then took flight to Glengarriff in County Cork for a memorable honeymoon.

The voice of the captain, and a gentle sinking feeling, woke me from my day dreams, and through the window I could see that we were losing height, and circling a palm-fringed coastline.

'Please check your seat belt. We are preparing to land at Davao.'

In the airport, there was a strong military presence — soldiers with rifles everywhere.

'Whatever you do, do not make eye contact — pretend that you don't see them and follow us.'

Cynthia and Romy led the way briskly and we passed through without incident. Soon we were shuddering and bumping on the unkempt surface of the crowded streets of Davao on the back of a ramshackle pick-up truck with bald tyres and no windscreen, taking in the sights, sounds and odours of the island of Mindanao. Fruit and vegetable stalls lined our route and hundreds of men and women, mostly barefoot, sauntered through the dust and litter while children, attracted by our white faces, raced alongside with hands outstretched looking for an offering,

'Hi Joe! You got money, Joe?'

The road was packed with vehicles, the vast majority of which were extremely old, and the most prominent were the jeepneys. These originated from the American jeeps that had been abandoned by United States military forces after the Second World War. The resourceful Filipinos enlarged and transformed them into brightly coloured minibuses, which reflected the religiosity of the people with boldly proclaimed titles of the Blessed Virgin and names of saints in gaudy lettering, while rosary beads and other pious objects adorned their cabs and windscreens. With young men and women hanging from the sides and sitting on the roof, they sped along, dodging and weaving, completely disregarding all the conventions of the road that we were used to. But in spite of that, we soon became aware that Filipinos are expert drivers — always travelling as fast as possible on their brakes and horns. The town was noisy, dusty and heavily polluted with exhaust fumes. Donkeys laden with firewood, tricycle taxis and barking dogs added to the clatter and commotion. It was pandemonium beyond all my expectations and to cap it all the temperature was in the nineties.

Given the state of the roads and the tyres on our vehicle, it was no surprise when a puncture brought us to a halt.

'Everybody out! We push to side of road.'

We jumped out, but were unable to get near the back end of the truck, for every child in creation had already arrived to assist. It became obvious that this was a frequent diversion for them, and when a space was found by the roadside to carry

A jeepney

out repairs, there was no shortage of unsolicited advice and voluntary labour from the menfolk. A huddle of women also gathered to enjoy the babble and chatter which accompanied the operation, and as ever, more children flocked to gaze into our pink faces, stroke the hairs on our arms inquisitively, and clean us out of all the sweets that we were carrying — and we roasted in the midday sun.

The operation, which had taken on the character of a social occasion, was eventually concluded with farewells and handshakes, and we continued the journey with a dozen or so children hanging on to the sides or perched on the roof. At their convenience, they jumped off regardless of speed like paratroopers in training, and an hour or so later we had left the town far behind, and for several kilometres we bounced through banana plantations, along a cart track by the shore, and eventually pulled into a compound where a large bamboo building resembling a barn stood on stilts on the silver sand amidst palm trees. Romy announced,

'This is our hotel.'

At first we thought this a joke, but we soon realised that this was indeed an hotel. Bare and sparsely furnished, it exuded frugality, but the welcome was warm and friendly and a table with rice, fish and fruit was awaiting our attention. On the seaward side the hotel was open to the breeze and birds fluttered above our heads while poultry scampered around our feet, and on the beach we could see a family of fisher folk working at their nets. It seemed like Shangri-la.

But we were soon to learn otherwise. After our meal, our hosts — highly organised as ever — presented us with our programme which began with a 'situationer':

'Mindanao has been called The Land Of Promise, but it is a land of promise denied to its people. As we travel around, you will see lots of fruit — bananas, pineapples, melons, mangoes, coconuts and much more in great abundance. There is also mineral wealth — gold, copper and nickel. But for the vast majority of its people Mindanao is an island of grinding poverty. The causes are many and complex, but at the heart of the matter is international debt. President Marcos has taken on massive loans from the banks and financial institutions of the rich nations of the West, and he and his cronies have lined their pockets and bank accounts. Interest rates have soared and in order to service these enormous debts multi-national companies have been brought in to take over our land to grow pineapples for export to the rich countries.

Thus the people have been dispossessed and thousands of families are now landless and homeless. The same is true of our mineral wealth and our forests, and even the fish around our shores are taken from us.

'You will see all this at first hand, for we shall visit coconut farmers who are at this very moment being brutally evicted, stay overnight with fisherfolk and hear their story, you will also stay with tribal Filipinos who have been driven from their forest homes by logging companies. We shall call on human rights workers and journalists who are constantly living under death threats because of their commitment to justice. There is some good news too, for we shall stay in a Basic Christian Community and experience something of the faith and solidarity of those who live, work pray and play together in the midst of persecution.'

In the late afternoon we swam in the warm waters

Fisherfolk in the South China Sea

of the South China Sea and in the evening under the stars we were introduced to the delights of San Miguel beer and talked into the night appraising all that had happened in so short a time. Then we climbed a bamboo ladder to a dormitory where fowls had already taken up positions in the rafters, and there we all slept (after a fashion) on the floor, Filipino style, wrapped only in cotton sheets and fanned by the soft sea breeze.

At first light, about 5.00 a.m., we came to life. Following the example of our hosts, we poured water over ourselves and each other, and then breakfasted on boiled rice and eggs. For the next two hours we bumped and bounced and jostled over roads that were mere dirt tracks and negotiated our way through streams. At times the drop into a gorge of several hundred feet might concentrate our minds and we looked again at the

A malnourished family about to be made destitute

bald tyres of our vehicle and agreed that it ceased to be a joke. But in spite of our anxieties and several bumps and bruises, the wonder of the unfamiliar — paddy fields and exotic plants — held our fascination until, turning off the main track, we pulled into a clearing where, in a cluster of bamboo huts, lived five coconut farmers with their families. They were the remnant of a larger community that after much harassment had abandoned their homes and livelihoods and moved on. Further down the track, we saw the smouldering remains of a family home and another being bulldozed. Fruit-bearing coconut trees were being uprooted and a young man was comforting his tearful wife — they had been married only two weeks previous to our visit. With the help of Cynthia and Romy, our facilitators and guides, we talked to the few remaining families. In turn they spoke in whispers:

> 'Soldiers come at night and knock on our doors. They ask for money. If we have none they attack us and kill our poultry.'

> 'Sometimes they rape our daughters and when our sons and husbands try to defend them, they knock them senseless with their rifle butts.'

> 'They took my daddy away and he has not come back.'

> 'Two days ago our 17-year-old son was tortured, where you are standing now. There was nothing we could do. They took him away and he has not returned. The rest of our young men have fled. They will join the N.P.A. and become terrorists.'

As they spoke, the women, looking much older

than their years, brushed away tears from their cheeks, while their husbands sat grim-faced, and small children, barefoot and dressed only in long shirts, gazed sadly into the faces of the strangers — and the 'strangers' were desperately trying to make sense of the whole sorry business.

'But why do the soldiers do this?'

'It is harassment. The Company pay them to do this so that they will break our spirits and we will flee. This saves the Company the trouble of having to evict us.'

Until a few days previous, I had lived in blissful ignorance, and therefore untroubled by the wretchedness of others. Now it seemed that I would never be quite the same again, and I reflected that at the heart of our Christian faith is the belief that we are all one body in Christ, therefore, their human rights are my human rights, their suffering my suffering and their persecution my persecution - that is what I understood by the term 'solidarity'.

We talked, made notes and took photographs late into the afternoon until the trees started to turn purple and our surroundings became flooded with shadows. Then, the sky took fire with the setting of the sun and the Philippines night followed quickly, but before the heavens began to sparkle, we were once more on the back of our truck and being shaken like peas in a castanet as we made our way to the bishop's house, where a warm welcome and iced San Miguel awaited our arrival. That night we slept soundly on mattresses in the seminary close by.

General Santos City

Our visit to fisherfolk next day was a happier affair. Ramshackle houses, now a familiar sight, were clustered around the bay close to General Santos City, where some fifty families lived more or less on top of one another. When we arrived, it seemed that everyone was on the quay doing nothing in particular, save socialising or washing themselves in public under a huge pipe that gushed water taken from a nearby stream, but soon we realised that they were all there to greet us. A smaller group, with a splash of formality, were the official welcoming party. Their leader, a young bearded Che Guevara look-a-like, stepped forward with outstretched hand.

'My name is Ricardo, the Barangay Captain.'

Romy, anxious that we might show due deference, added,

'He is the community leader, elected by the people.'

Ricardo was a bright, handsome and attractive personality, and he spoke good English too.

'Welcome. We hope that you will enjoy your visit. Everyone looks forward to meeting you, so we have arranged a reception with snacks, and then afterwards we shall go on walkabout. Please come this way.'

We were led to a large, three-sided shed — their fish market by day and social centre, theatre, and basket-ball pitch in the evening, where a line of trestle tables awaited our attention. It was clearly a case of 'family hold back', for hundreds of barefoot children with smiling faces and expectant eyes lined the route. I took a swift glance at the mountain of rice and a scattering of small fish.

'Surprise, surprise,' I whispered, 'but I'd sell my grannie for a nice cuppa and a bacon buttie.'

The remark struck a sympathetic chord in one or two hearts, for a mild explosion of laughter relieved the formality among my male colleagues, which in turn produced a puzzled smile on the faces of our hosts. Bhavana, who was not amused, shot a disapproving glance in my direction, but her rebuke was gentle:

'Vin, did I hear correctly?'

She was right to chastise — it was an unworthy thought, and a moment's reflection made me ponder the preparation and sacrifice that must have been made by these poor fisherfolk in order to welcome us as guests of honour.

After we had eaten, some young men performed a splendid dramatic presentation and, though it was in a foreign tongue, we had no difficulty understanding its theme — a moving depiction of their plight and struggle for justice. This was followed by the promised walkabout with Ricardo living up to all our expectations. He was interesting, articulate and thankfully brief, for the midday heat was by now once again sapping our energy. His analysis of the problems facing his community was nonetheless thorough:

'Of course, we lack the basic necessities —

sanitation, access to clean water, adequate housing and health care, but at the heart of all our problems is the reality that our fish is being stolen from our waters.'

We were standing by the shore as he spoke and, pointing to a very large vessel beyond the bay, he continued:

'That is a fishing boat from Japan. But it is not just a fishing boat. It is also a factory, for the fish are caught in very fine nets, processed and canned on the boat, and then taken to be sold in other countries far from these islands. Our little boats go out each day but often return as vessels of despair, for there is very little left for us and our livelihood is being taken away. Sometimes we experience real hunger.'

The conversation for the next few hours was heavy and serious, so in the evening, ready to relax, we

Families watch their livelihood taken by Japanese fishing boat

sat near the shore by torchlight, told our jokes, sang our songs to guitar accompaniment and talked into the night, after which we were privileged to sleep on the floor in the homes of poor fishermen and their families.

At sunrise I was up and about — so was everyone else. I enjoyed watching the barrio (village) come to life. I had learned to love this place in so short a time, with its pitted paths, open drains, skinny dogs and scabby cats; its silent elders sitting by their doorways smoking; its womenfolk engaged in public acts of domesticity — feeding the baby, washing clothes and carrying water — all in the mixed aroma of woodsmoke and fish boxes. But it was time to move on.

After the meal one enjoys a pipe

T'boli family home

South Cotabato

In South Cotabato we were entertained by the T'boli tribe. A large gathering - all in colourful traditional dress - welcomed us with music and dance. Later, as guests of honour, we sat in a circle on rush mats to share what was, to all intents and purposes, a veritable banquet and colourful display of fruit, vegetables, meat and rice. The chief's home was a large bamboo hut on stilts accommodating twenty to thirty guests, but many more, adults as well as children, looked on as spectators, climbing the walls and peering through the windows. They were transfixed as they gazed at the strange creatures who had come to visit them. The chief, wishing to explain their interest, spoke to us in halting English.

'We .. never .. have .. visitors .. from .. other .. countries, .. so .. everyone .. comes .. to .. look .. at .. you.'

'Is it because of the colour of our skin, or the way we speak?'

He was silent for a few moments and then with artless candour said,

'Yes, .. but .. it .. is .. also .. your .. big .. noses.'

He laughed and we laughed and so did the audience, but clearly, not everyone understood the joke.

Rice was served to us on banana leaves and we were invited to take some meat. In a basket I could see chicken heads and wings — I opted for a wing, and spent the next few minutes picking the bones and, following their lead, ate rice with my fingers. I then tried some unidentifiable vegetables, before being pressed to sample what was obviously their speciality. Though with little enthusiasm, good manners dictated that I should accept — after all it seemed to be well cooked — but as I munched the bland, tough meat, I thought that I detected a mischievous exchange of smiles between Romy and Cynthia, while my colleagues displayed a strong preference for rice and vegetables.

Later, we fell upon the tropical fruits with great delight and slaked our thirst with coconut juice. During all this time, conversation and translation went at a pace without a lull and, in the shadows, a duo with large bamboo pipes and a strange stringed instrument played weird background music. After taking our leave, Cynthia asked if we had enjoyed the meal.

'Oh yes, but not just the food. The whole cultural experience was quite exceptional.'

'Vin, did you enjoy the special meat dish?'

'Yes, but you laughed then and you're laughing now. What's so funny?'

'It was dog.'

'No, you're pulling my leg.'

'But I don't touch your leg.'

'I mean you are joking. Tell me you are joking. It was not dog .... was it?'

Romy interjected and confirmed that it was indeed dog that I had eaten:

'Yes, truly that was dog. It was black dog — that is very special.'

Her face had now taken on a serious aspect and I knew that she was speaking the truth. As for my colleagues, they were convulsed with laughter.

We learned of the suffering's of the T'boli people in general and of how they had become dispossessed, but this particular community seemed now to be living rather well by comparison, and our next stop — a visit to the mission — explained all. A larger than life American priest showed us around his little world — a fine church building with presbytery, a large well equipped school, a clinic and well stocked dispensary, and not a sign of malnutrition anywhere. Our first reaction was one of amazement and then of puzzlement, for these amenities would not have been out of place in any developed country — but here in the Philippines outback, some explanation was called for.

'It is true that, relatively speaking, we live rather well here.'

After what we had seen in other places, that was quite an understatement, and we conjectured among ourselves how all this could have been achieved by one man.

'It's all a matter of money, isn't it. Back in the States my family and friends are very wealthy and they fund me. Whatever I ask for, within reason, I get.'

He had a warm, friendly and outgoing personality and was understandably very proud of his achievements, but there was something about his style and the atmosphere of the place that prompted us to question things — was it paternalism, a culture of dependency and a lack of 'get up and go' in the people? Certainly, there was widespread lethargy, which in other places we might have associated with malnutrition, so as we were bumped and bounced along more tracks and over more potholes to our next port of call, we discussed the pros and cons of some forms of missionary activity

and the nature of good development. Romy and Cynthia beamed satisfaction.

'That was the purpose of this visit — to challenge you to think about your partnership with the poor, for we don't want just any kind of development, and at any price. We want to sing our own song; we want liberation for our people.'

Basic Christian Community

It was early evening and black dark when we spilled out of the truck and started picking our way hesitantly along a narrow forest path. Then happily in the distance we saw flaming torches approaching and heard a babble of conversation. It was a picturesque meeting in woodland by torchlight — the flames picking out bronze faces

'The children greeted us with smiles'

and wispy black beards against a background of coconut and banana trees. Then turning, with their torches held high, the farmers led the way through what appeared to be a luxuriant plantation. Soon the smell of a wood fire and the sweet tang of cooking told us that we were approaching our destination, and then, it was like a festival of light that greeted us, for bottles, half buried in the soil and half filled with paraffin with pieces of rolled up rag, serving as wicks, made a flare path to guide our footsteps to a large bamboo house with an open kitchen. Tall flames were licking several large black cauldrons, adding domesticity to resplendence and bestowing a warm glow on the faces of twenty or so men, women and children who welcomed us with music and song. The place oozed happiness — it was a Basic Christian Community.

The Basic Christian Community ideal is as old as Christianity itself, but in more recent times has been greatly influenced by the Church's 'preferential option for the poor' in Latin America. The Philippines situation is different, but the response very much the same — the people share their work and they share the fruits of their work. Almost all of their few possessions are regarded as common property. They live, work, play and pray together. Sharing is an essential part of their lives - they share their Gospel reflection too, their faith insights and even their leadership.

We only stayed one night and half of the next day. It was not long enough, but in that short time we heard the now familiar stories of families who had been dispossessed; and then, under the leadership of a young Filipino priest, whose vision of the Gospel was one of liberation, they told us how they were brought together to form a community which truly became 'good news to the poor' — and to us it became, good news from the poor. We shared a meal, which despite its simplicity seemed like a feast because of the joy engendered by the people around the table. But most of all we 'sat in' on their bible reflection. It was clear that they had become expert at seeing special significance in certain scriptural passages which they applied with ease to their own situation. A young man wearing a T-shirt which

The Caribao - farmers' best friend and always a young lad's responsibility

Harvesting rice

proclaimed 'Lay Liturgical Leader' was eager to demonstrate how they related these key texts to their own condition.

'When we read the story of Exodus in the Old Testament, we see that a slave rabble, who were nobodies in the eyes of the world, were of great value in the eyes of God, who saved them through a political experience of liberation. We learn today what the Israelites learned then, that oppression is political and social sin.

'We sing the psalms, which are some of the great prayers of the People of God. They also teach us that God is the great liberator from the evils of oppression. In the New Testament, Jesus, at the very beginning of His public life reads from the scroll in the synagogue.

"The spirit of the Lord is upon me, for he has anointed me. He has sent me to bring good news to the poor, to heal the broken-hearted, to proclaim liberty to captives, freedom to those in prison."

'This gives us great heart for we know that we are important in the sight of God.'

The next day, still tousled with sleep, we walked in the early morning sun. There were chickens and children everywhere and all exercising their vocal chords to celebrate a new day. We helped feed the pigs, gathered firewood, carried water and played basketball, after a fashion — and all before 6.00a.m! After breakfast, we toured their paddy fields, where harvesting was already in progress, and young boys were leading massive caribous (water buffaloes) pulling wooden cart-loads of grain to the barn. Women in picturesque broadbrimmed headgear and scarves hanging loosely to their shoulders stood in circles chattering whilst winnowing the golden grain. At

Waving goodbye to the Basic Christian Community

noon, the blistering heat brought everyone indoors to drink, eat a little rice and sleep for a couple of hours, after which we said our goodbyes, retraced our steps through the forest and returned by truck to Davao City.

Alex Orcullo

It was our last full day on the island of Mindanao with only two items left to complete our programme, one a meeting with Alex Orcullo, and the second a visit to a Justice and Peace office. It was mid-morning when we arrived at our proposed rendezvous with Alex, at the office of CAFOD's partner agency near the centre of town. We were in high spirits, for everything had gone well and the next day we would be flying back to Manila to share our experiences with our friends and colleagues, and we had lots to tell. I well remember the banter and laughter as we awaited some reaction to our knock on the door. There was no immediate response, so we tried again. How could I ever forget what followed? A young woman opened the door and in a matter of fact way asked,

'Haven't you heard the news? Alex was salvaged yesterday.'

' Salvaged?'

'That's what we say when someone has been murdered by the military.'

'But why should the military do that?'

'Church workers, human rights workers — in fact anyone interested in justice — is perceived

to be a subversive and is often salvaged. But please come in.'

Inside, the table was laid with cold drinks and light snacks, and on the wall, rather appropriately we thought, was a poster depicting three bleeding bodies — one hanging from a tree, and the other two lying dead on the ground. The caption read,

'Blessed are those who are persecuted for the cause of justice, for theirs is the kingdom of heaven.'

We sat down in a daze, while our Filipino hosts seemed to get on with 'business as usual'.

'Please, merienda is served — would you like cold drinks and snacks?'

We pondered and whispered to one another,

'Why aren't these Filipinos distressed? It seems that we are more concerned than they are.'

Our stage whispers were not ignored.

'We do care. But you really must realise that this is an everyday occurrence for us and, unless it is a very close friend or relative, we get on with our lives. But it really does hurt. Please understand that we live in a climate of fear — especially those of us who are working for justice, or who are in solidarity with the poor.'

'Tell us about Alex.'

'He was a councillor and a journalist who wrote about human rights issues. He had received death threats, so some weeks ago for safety, he left town with his family to stay with friends.

'Yesterday was his thirty-ninth birthday and,

thinking that it might be safe, he returned home. He stopped to buy vegetables at a market. A military vehicle pulled up beside him. He was ordered to get out of his car and he was simply pumped with bullets in front of his wife and five children.'

Cora and Jose

The Justice and Peace office was in the heart of Davao City. Cora, a tiny young woman of about twenty years of age, petite and pretty, but with a maturity beyond her years, and her assistant, Jose, a young man of seventeen, ran this tiny bureau. It was in reality no more than a documentation centre for missing persons and for those who had been salvaged, and was frequented mainly by women enquiring about their missing sons or husbands. Few people have impressed me more than Cora, the tiny Filipino, for her commitment and maturity, but especially for her bravery.

Her cabinets were full to overflowing with files containing detailed notes and photographs relating to corpses that had been found by the roadside, or floating in the river.

'My work is mainly in this office, keeping records and answering queries about missing persons. Jose goes out with his motor cycle and camera each day to bring back the evidence.'

'Is that a full-time job?'

'Oh, yes, on average, five bodies are picked out of the river each day.'

'Who are they? What have they done?'

'All kinds of people — mostly men, but sometimes women are salvaged too. They are nearly always people who are opposed to the Marcos dictatorship, but sometimes the military make mistakes, because they are not efficient. Trades Unionists and Church Workers are especially at risk - people like Alex Orcullo. Did you hear about him?'

'Yes we did — we were to meet him this morning. But what about you? Aren't you also at risk?'

At this point in our conversation, Cora looked at me and paused, no doubt considering my pathetic question, and then this tough, brave young woman broke down and wept. I swallowed hard as I felt the tears welling up in my own eyes. I wanted to hug her but I could not — I left that to the women folk. She reminded me so much of my own daughter, Rosanne, of much the same age, who was up to her neck in left-wing politics, openly opposed to the Government of the day, but all in the context and safety of a democratic nation.

'You ask if I am at risk. Already, I have received four death threats, and they have now told me that I am top of their list.'

It was time for us to move on, but how could we do that? It seemed unthinkable that we could shake her hand, wish her well, assure her of our prayers and then walk away. But what could we do? We were all very moved — some of us to tears. It was Cynthia who took charge of the situation:

'I think that we should take lunch in a restaurant today and Cora will be our guest.'

Just then Jose appeared with his morning's work

— more photographs and statements to be processed — but we did not have the stomach to peruse them. Instead, we invited him also to lunch; he took little persuasion. Before we left the office, Cora gave a cautionary word of advice;

'When we step outside, you will notice that there are people loitering on the street - not all are innocent bystanders, so please don't speak and make no eye contact.'

Given the numbers on the busy thoroughfare, it would have been difficult, in any case, to identify anyone with sinister intent, so, following instructions, we weaved and jostled our way to our rendezvous, where four wheels whisked us away to a restaurant on the edge of town.

It was just what we had come to expect, basic and functional, without any unnecessary decoration or furniture. We gathered around a bare table close to the kitchen, drinking beer and enjoying the rich aroma of cooking and wood smoke, and in spite of what had gone before, lunch was a relaxed and happy affair. The tears of an hour or so earlier were forgotten, the conversation was peppered with jokes ancient and modern, and the food was delicious too. It was good therapy all round, but all too soon it was time to say our goodbyes, and Cora and Jose, looking younger and more vulnerable than ever, scurried away, then turning, gave a brief wave, and disappeared among the masses.

Just when we thought our programme was complete we were unexpectedly blessed with another interesting visit — an invitation into the home of Karl Gasper's mother. Karl, a Church worker and one of CAFOD's partners, was in Davao Prison and currently on Amnesty's list of prisoners of conscience. We had been unable to visit him in prison, so to be able to accept the warm hospitality of his mother was a privilege indeed.

Parliament Of The Streets

That evening as we packed our bags and prepared for our departure next day, Romy came with some news,

'The unions, backed by the N.P.A., have called a general strike. No wheels must turn tomorrow.'

'Does that refer to all transport?'

'Yes, it means everything.'

'Can they impose this?'

'Yes, and they will. It would be suicidal to defy them.'

'So that means that we cannot leave tomorrow?'

'That's right, unless I am able to negotiate a permit — permission to take you to the airport in our truck. Of course, the airport will function as normal.'

It seemed obvious to me that Romy spoke with some confidence and had something up her sleeve - influence in high places perhaps - and I was very hopeful that some concession would be made. I also noted that our hosts seemed to be smiling a lot - was it all a leg pull, or was it that they welcomed this crisis as a fitting end to our Exposure Programme?

However, there were not many smiles the next morning. Everyone was tense, for though permission had been granted, there was a whiff of danger in the air. A length of bamboo cane to serve as a flag-pole was secured to our vehicle, on which was tied a piece of white cloth and, so that there would be no mistaking our peaceful intent, we were all asked to hold aloft our handkerchiefs.

What an eerie atmosphere pervaded the town that morning! There were none of the customary noises — no hooting and honking of horns and ringing of bells and no traffic jams. The streets were almost deserted, until the noise of our engine attracted attention, and then, people ran out and lined our route in silence and looked expectantly in our direction. It was as if they had rushed out to witness some fireworks.

We moved slowly along the main street of Davao and then we were stopped at a road block where men with rifles and in para-military dress came to check us out. Romy handed them a piece of paper, which they scrutinised while we held our breath. They walked around the truck eyeing us closely, and then they did the same again, jabbering to Romy and Cynthia and to each other. Eventually, they sent us on our way with a smile and a wave, and we heaved a sigh of relief — not so much because we had felt threatened, but because by now we were looking forward to our return flight to Manila and the reunion with the rest of our colleagues. Only one more road block delayed us before arriving at Davao Airport with two hours to spare before take-off.

Sitting in the frugal comfort of the Airport lounge, and later at a height of more than 20,000 feet, we reviewed our experiences of the past week or so — it seemed much longer, for we had packed so much into such a short time. We chattered non-stop, chewed over every detail and scribbled into notebooks until fatigue mercifully took prisoners and, one by one, heads nodded, eyelids closed, and then, all senses lulled by the sonorous whirr of the aircraft's engines, we surrendered to a deep sleep.

Manila was her usual self — hot, sticky, heavily polluted and noisy. The city centre, congested with traffic, at times almost to a complete standstill, and child beggars, some of them blind or deformed, everywhere. They tapped relentlessly on our taxi window to attract attention and I reflected how much easier it had become, in such a short time, to ignore their pleas.

It was a slow, tiresome journey to the convent in the blistering heat of midday but eventually we arrived to a cheerful reception. Everyone bursting to tell their stories — of living with tribal people in the north of Luzon, standing with workers on picket lines, attending the trial of Ed. de la Torres, a priest accused of subversive activities, and visiting Manila's infamous rubbish dump, Smokey Mountain, where thousands of families live and scavenge for a living. We spent two days sharing, debriefing and evaluating our experiences and then we walked with workers, families of detainees and priests and nuns in demonstrations and protest marches, which had been given the title, 'Parliament Of The Streets'. These events were the vanguard of the massive uprising which was to take place less than two years later — the revolution which overthrew the vicious dictator, President Marcos and swept Cory Aquino into power.

At the end of our programme in Manila we had an audience with Cardinal Sin:

'Welcome to the house of Sin', and that was very much the tone of his contribution — light-hearted and friendly, but though generous with his time, he steered clear of any serious social comment, let alone analysis.

On our last evening in the Philippines we celebrated the Eucharist, after which a valedictory shindig erupted when, fortified with San Miguel, we sang our songs, recited poetry and told jokes well into the night. Then a little formality seemed appropriate and votes of thanks were proposed and gifts exchanged, but our hosts had the last word:

'When you go home, please tell our story.'

With a jumble of emotions, we said our individual goodbyes and then turned in to sleep fitfully for the last time on a bamboo floor. It was now all over and my thoughts and dreams during that last night centred on home and family, in another world, just 36 hours away.

Mindanao — A land of promise

FAMINE

'I can't close my eyes at night without being haunted
by the face of a starving child.' — *Cardinal Basil Hume.*

England looked its beautiful best through a hazy morning sun. The countryside and suburban gardens were clothed in russet and red, a carpet of crisp leaves crunched underfoot, there was an agreeable frosty nip in the air and an autumn scent of woodsmoke to greet me on my return. I was back home. The trip, from start to finish, had been truly a wondrous experience, but nevertheless, it was good to be back in familiar surroundings, and I was more appreciative than ever of the comforts of a bed and an armchair, water (hot and cold) at the turn of a tap, and a home where I basked in the prattle and hurly-burly of family life.

'Dad you don't half look skinny. You've lost your belly.'

'What was the food like?'

'Did you have rice with every meal? .... No bread? ....No spuds?'

'How hot was it?'

'Did you really enjoy it?'

'How long were you in the aeroplane?'

Rosanne, who had been holding fire and waiting her opportunity to get a word in, announced,

'Wait till you see the news on television — the most horrific famine in Ethiopia.'

I had returned from the Philippines with an agenda that I had prepared for myself, but everything was to change. Julian, CAFOD's Director, had warned me of an impending famine in Africa, but nothing could have prepared me for the scale of the tragedy. It turned out to be the biggest disaster in living memory and for the first time, courtesy of television, people were witnessing, night after night, children dying in their thousands. Of course, we had all seen, many times before, sad faces and pot bellies, but this was quite different, and the numbers were staggering — thousands of walking skeletons, and close-ups of babies crawling over the empty breasts of their dead mothers, while others lay motionless in the dust, covered with flies and breathing their last silent gasp — and all this viewed from the comfort of our living rooms.

Not surprisingly, Church leaders, Government Ministers, 'showbiz' personalities and others prominent in public life, visited the stricken areas to show solidarity with the suffering masses. There was also good-natured competition among the various agencies to capture the attention of the media — the all-important photo calls and sound bytes on radio and television. As is well known, Bob Geldof also visited Ethiopia and did much to raise awareness of the scale and causes of the tragedy, but will be forever remembered as the inspiration and driving force of a massive fundraising initiative — Live Aid.

As for me, I had hardly recovered from jet lag when I too was caught up in what must have been the most amazing response ever from the British public, and I felt honoured to be a small part of it. For the past twenty-five years I had enjoyed my work as a teacher — fifteen as headteacher — but now, in spite of being run off my feet, I experienced such a deep sense of privilege that I woke up every morning with a smile on my face.

Despite massive unemployment in Liverpool, my tiny room in the Curial Offices became inundated with donations — a sack of mail was dropped on my desk every morning, and the phone never stopped:

'Can you come to Assembly, say a few words about the famine, and we'll present you with a cheque?'

'We've collected two thousand pounds. Can you come tomorrow and pick it up — we've got the press lined up for ten o' clock?'

'Radio Merseyside here. Are you available for interview at 7.30 in the morning and tell us the latest from Ethiopia — with a local link if possible?'

'Father Peter, Holy Family parish, here. Could you come and speak at the Masses on Sunday?'

Speaking at Masses was quite a daunting prospect, but I was not coming to the world of public speaking as a complete beginner — in fact I could perhaps have been described as somewhat accomplished, for I had received excellent training and experience with the Catholic Evidence Guild. That was in the pre-Vatican Council era, when every Friday evening I had attended a study class and every Sunday evening, for several years, had taken my turn as a 'soap box' orator in Newcastle's Bigg Market, engaging in the polemics of Catholic doctrine with atheists, agnostics, and, in those days before ecumenism had entered our vocabulary, with fellow Christians too, whom we called, in our more charitable mood, 'separated brethren'. How many times have I recalled those heady days when, fortified with a memory bank stuffed to overflowing with 'Sheehan's Apologetics', I savoured the cut and thrust of open air debate, taking as my role model the inspirational Frank Sheed. He and his devoted wife, Maisie Ward, were co-founders of the Guild.

But speaking in this context was different. For a start there was no audible heckling, but one felt that at least some of the faithful understandably resented a layperson assuming the role of the priest in the pulpit, so with that in mind, I usually 'played away from home', where there would be fewer, '*who does he think he is*', comments to distract me from the serious and onerous task of informing, edifying and appealing to the consciences of my fellow Catholics.

Still, the requests continued and happily the money poured in. Processing cash and cheques took priority, for we were becoming submerged under a tidal wave of generosity. And the telephone kept ringing.

> 'Nora O'Shaughnessy here. I bet you're busy. Can I give a hand?'

> 'You can give two hands; I'm snowed under. There must be more than a thousand pounds on my desk just waiting for an angel like you to count and get off to the bank.'

> 'I'm on my way'.

A knock on the door — Mike Merriman had arrived unheralded.

> 'Sit down, Mike, you've got a job.'

Just then what sounded like a mild disturbance on the stairs caused us to pause and listen.

> 'You can't bring that in here!'

> 'Yes we can. We've pushed it for twenty bloody miles, so a few stairs won't beat us.... and don't

stand there looking at us — give a hand.'

> 'Hey, watch the paintwork.... and be careful or you'll do yourself an injury.'

The sound of footsteps running along the corridor gave us more cause for concern and we were about to involve ourselves when the office door burst open. A large pram of yesteryear made an entry followed by two exhausted but triumphant women.

> 'What the hell....?'

> 'How's that for a street collection?'

We could hardly believe our eyes. It was full to overflowing, bursting at its seams, with money!

> 'Mike and Nora, your arrival couldn't have been timed better. Let's get to work.'

The next day a knock on the door heralded a less dramatic entry. Dressed in boiler suit and cloth cap, a short, stocky, middle-aged man hesitated for an instant and then placed a neat package on the desk and made an exit as abrupt as his entry.

> 'Hey come back - what's all this?'

By this time, I was following him down the stairs. Clearly, he wanted no fuss and kept walking as he replied,

> 'It's clean. I've just got it out the bank — £1,000. After what I saw on television last night that money doesn't belong to me, so no fuss, please.'

There was much more. An avalanche of giving had visited the nation, and the clergy joined in

Vin in St. Sylvester's Infant School, Liverpool.

Photo: Carlos Reyes

Cardinal Basil Hume, wearing one of Vin's T-shirts, and flanked by Cathy Corcoran, Project Officer for Ethiopia, with Julian Filochowski, CAFOD's Director.

Photo: Carlos Reyes

the dance — though some were pushed. I was called to parishes all over the country to pick up huge cheques. And the telephone calls continued.

'Mine is a very poor parish in Stockport — a run-down council estate with too many problems of its own — not least more than fifty per cent unemployment rate. It would give them a boost if you could come — they did it all themselves.'

I was rocked on my heels to receive from poor people a cheque for two thousand pounds. That was a huge sum in those days, but in this context, it was obvious that people had given not from their spare cash (they did not have any), but truly from their substance. The experience reinforced what I had always known — it is not always those that have the most who give the most.

Senior clergy gave great prophetic witness too, and Cardinal Hume wasted little time in visiting Ethiopia accompanied by Julian and Cathy Corcoran, CAFOD's project officer.

'Vin, get half a dozen T-shirts on the London train today. We're flying out tomorrow.'

We were becoming ever more conscious of the need to promote CAFOD's name as a real player in the unfolding drama. In Liverpool, Archbishop Worlock and his Anglican counterpart, Bishop David Sheppard, had no difficulty in capturing the headlines, sound bytes and photo opportunities. Auxiliary Bishop Tony Hitchen, CAFOD's Chairman, was busy working himself to death with an agenda superimposed on an already full pastoral programme. He supported

all my endeavours with great good humour and generosity of spirit — not least The CAFOD Christmas Run. This was regarded by many to be 'One of Vin's hare-brained initiatives.'

'A Sponsored Run at Christmas?...... Nobody will come...... It's the wrong time...... Who will leave their fireside to run in mud or snow?'

But I felt that it was just the right time — the very time in fact that many people would want to share, out of their Christmas excess, with the poorest people in the world — and Tony Hitchen agreed:

'Go for it, Vin. I think you're right — and you can call on me.'

'What to run?'

'Not b..... likely but I'll be your official starter.'

It was November and there was little time to prepare for a big event to be held on the Sunday between Christmas and New Year, and I was about to throw myself into it when I was called to London.

'Vin, Julian here. I want you to drop everything and come to Head Office for a couple of weeks.'

'What's all this? I'm snowed under here.'

'Yes, I know, but so are we, and we're under enormous pressure. There is to be a Disasters Emergency Committee Appeal for the famine and it's our turn to administer it. All are working flat out and we're recruiting volunteers. I wouldn't ask if it wasn't so important.'

'Let me think this over — there are family

considerations, of course, and I'd need to organise volunteers at this end too. I'll let you know.'

Two days later, I was on the early train to Euston.

It was a heady atmosphere at Head Office — especially in the upstairs corridors where an aura of quiet excitement had taken hold, not unrelated to media attention on this whole famine-relief operation, while in the Committee Room on the ground floor a dozen or so volunteers and a few CAFOD staff sat around tables, formed into a hollow square, and prattled as they performed repetitive tasks — opening envelopes, sorting cheques and writing receipts — and where a two-year-old provided a welcome distraction, crawling around feet, pulling shoelaces and wiping sticky fingers on skirts and trousers.

I worked around that table from early morning till early evening — and then into the night with Julian and Nigel to clear the decks for next day. CAFOD's own income increased enormously. There was an upsurge of euphoria and the adrenaline flowed as we began to realise that we were no longer small fry on the Charities scene with only two dozen full-time staff, but were becoming a real player in this unfolding drama and making a unique contribution through our worldwide Church network. The tidal wave of generosity swept us along with little time for reflection, and I recall the cautionary words of a wise monk:

'Agencies rarely get better by becoming bigger.'

Those in the Education Department agreed with those sentiments and they considered it far more important that we should concern ourselves with the raising of awareness and getting the British government to face up to its responsibilities, than simply with the raising of funds. The problem of world poverty, we were constantly reminded, was so massive that it could not be solved by all the agencies put together, however efficient and well meaning. It required the transferring of funds on a huge scale from the developed world to the developing world — thus only governments could solve the problem, and education was the key. Inevitably, there was some tension between the 'purists' in the Education Department and the pragmatists in the Appeals Department. As the first and only member of staff working in the regions, I could have been assigned to either department, but at the insistence of Julian and Bishop Hitchen, I had been placed in the Appeals Department. Nevertheless, I felt that I had a foot in both camps, and when the opportunity presented itself, I made my contribution to the debate with what I considered to be a statement of the obvious, and advocated an integrated approach:

'We must integrate: fund-raising without which we cannot exist, awareness-raising without which we are not really part of the solution, campaigning without which we are not in true solidarity with the poor and oppressed and spirituality without which we are mere humanists.'

On my return to Liverpool, I threw myself into all aspects of CAFOD's work.

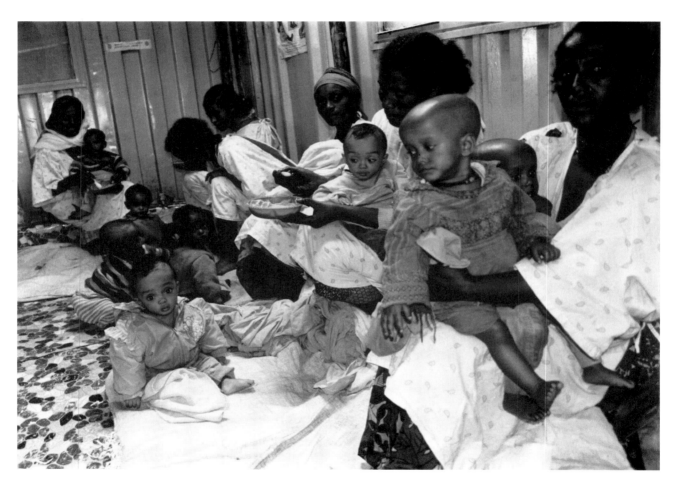

Mothers with malnourished children — Feeding Station in Addis Ababa

Christmas '84

'O Little Town Of Bethlehem
How still we see thee lie ....'

The Salvation Army brass band and a handful of sopranos and tenors were giving forth in the Station forecourt and once more nourishing the festive atmosphere with carols and Christian witness, while crowded streets and busy shopping malls were telling a different story of commercialism and consumerism gone mad.

It was the weekend before Christmas and multicoloured parcels and packages of every shape and size seemed to glide along pavements with men, women and children attached, while Christmas trees took to shuffling through congested thoroughfares, and boisterous youths called excitedly to one another over the traffic's noise.

As usual, there was a superabundance of frippery — streamers, holly and mistletoe everywhere — while animated plastic Santas and snowy-backed reindeers nodded and waved from shop windows.

Inside the big store, Father Christmas, hidden from view in the deep recesses of his grotto, was doing a roaring trade, and outside, barrow boys with cartloads of fruit competed vigorously for a share of the takings amidst a yuletide aroma of roasting chestnuts.

As the afternoon wore on, the 'real Santa', throned on high (courtesy of the Round Table) on the back of a decorated float arrived with great ceremony to switch on the town's Christmas illuminations to a chorus of 'oohs and aahs' from the young and not so young. The spirit of Christmas had been released:

'Happy Christmas.... Many o' them....'

'And the compliments of the season to you too.'

'Isn't it lovely for the young-uns.'

But here and there yet another story was being told. A poster appeared in one or two shop windows, showing a suffering, yet dignified, Ethiopian mother with her malnourished baby, reminiscent of a classical Madonna and Child painting. It struck a different note. But this was no mere exercise in artistic appreciation — this was for real — a photograph that had been taken a matter of a few weeks previously, an image of a real mother and a real baby destined to die by hunger in a world that has too much food — a challenge to the conscience of our affluent society that was spending millions of pounds on Christmas excesses. And Christians might well have pondered the words of the Magnificent song of Mary:

'He hath filled the hungry with good things and the rich He hath sent empty away.'

The caption on the poster read, *'Lord When Did We See You Hungry'*.

And yet in spite of all that, it seemed to me that a feeling of guilt was quite the wrong response — the right response was to share, not the spare coppers left over after a night out, but from one's substance, and to campaign for justice in our world. Then we shall indeed have something to celebrate — our solidarity with the poor, and we shall look to the prophecy of Isaiah:

'On this mountain the Lord of hosts will make for all peoples a feast of rich food, a feast of well aged-wines....'

There were a number of happy faces on street corners, flag day volunteers shaking their tins and placing *Famine in Africa Appeal* stickers on the lapels of donors. From department stores piped music rang out with the Christmas number one, by Bob Geldof, *'Do They Know It's Christmas?'*.

Having been moved by television pictures of widespread suffering in Ethiopia, Geldof, who was leader of 'Boomtown Rats', established the pop charity, 'Band Aid', which, during the Christmas period was to raise eight million pounds for African famine relief from the sales of a single record.

Throughout the land thousands of others were moved to celebrate Christmas a little differently that year. One priest exhorted his people to calculate all their Christmas expenditure and then to give ten per cent of the total to the poorest people in the world. Thus, the sum of ten thousand pounds was raised for African famine relief in just one parish; and, to increase awareness, Mary, Joseph and their baby were depicted as a homeless family fleeing for their lives as refugees to a foreign land. Meeting Jesus in the poor became the challenge for many Christians, but on the whole consumerism and nativity scenes continued to co-exist side by side without too many people noticing the contradiction, and come Christmas, everyone celebrated as usual with carols, Midnight Masses and revelry and we over-ate, overdrank and partied. Then, with Christmas behind us, with the help of sturdy volunteers, I had a job to do.

It was the post Christmas hibernation period and a cold dark morning, too early for even the faintest hint of dawn in the December sky, and visibility was poor. Nevertheless, I caught the occasional glimpse of hoar frost in the hedgerows, and the tarmac sparkled along country lanes in my headlights' beam — otherwise, not a glimmer of light, save the occasional flicker of a Christmas tree through a frosted window, and it was a silent world. Who would have chosen to venture forth at such an early hour on such a morning? Surely the whole of creation had opted to remain curled up in comfort — except for me. Was this a hare-brained idea after all? Would anyone turn up? Yes, I could count on the faithful team of volunteers who had already given much time to assist in the preparation and planning of the event, but even they — were they convinced that it would be a success? My mind was in turmoil. I had hardly slept. Time and again I went over my tick list — stewards and car park attendants, first aid, insurance, police, ropes, cones, stakes, arrows, signs, and banners .... etc. etc. But I kept asking myself the same question,

'Will anyone turn up — will the whole enterprise be a well-publicised flop?'

Upholland College was the venue, and as I turned into the drive, the car skidded to the left then to the right and finally came to a halt facing the wrong way. Salt and sand — why had I forgotten to put them on the list? I had better give that matter some priority, and just then I noted a faint crack of sunlight on the horizon and my spirits rose. Perhaps nature would be kind and solve the problem with a rise in temperature by noon. As I approached the main entrance I met Monsignor John Butchard, the College Director, already up and about and taking no chances, spreading grit on the forecourt.

'Good morning, Vin, what were the roads like?'

'Not good, but not too bad either. I'm hopeful — the sun will be cracking the flagstones by dinner time.'

'The eternal optimist! But that would be a mixed blessing anyway. Remember the cars will be parking on grass — you want firm ground. How many are you expecting?'

'That's the sixty-four-thousand-dollar question. We've got a couple of hundred entries — if they turn up — and lots more said they'd register on the day. Given the weather it's anybody's guess. There'll be spectators too, of course, but who knows how many?'

'Well, I'm running, so that's one definite anyway.'

'And I'm running, so that's two - a huge sporting event!'

I was trying my best to sound relaxed and confident, but inside my stomach was turning at the thoughts of a possible fiasco.

Two hours later volunteers were busying themselves with a thousand tasks in bright sunshine. Peter Callaghan, the course Director, with his wife, Sheila, and Ged Corcoran, a surgeon at a Liverpool hospital, were marking the course and roping off the finish. Mike Merriman was putting up signs, John Clarke and family preparing hot drinks and refreshments, Tony Redmond, Jim McCauley, Austin Hughes and Harry Wallace stewarding the car park, and by midday everything was taking on the appearance of a well organised event with a huge banner indicating, 'The Start' and a brass band playing carols underneath. I was being pulled in every direction as families and school groups, a few serious looking athletes, a sprinkling of clergy and even one or two nuns in track suits, started to arrive.

'Where do we register?'

'The Red Cross ambulance is here. They want to know where to park.'

'Have you got any safety pins for my number?'

'What time does the Run start?'

'Where are the toilets, please?'

'Are there any refreshments for sale?'

'A coach has arrived and they want to know where they can park?'

'We are Catholic Women's League. Are we allowed to walk the course?'

'Bishop Hitchen's here — at the College entrance.'

'Do you have easy access to toilets for the disabled?'

'Vin, we're short of course stewards. Can you recruit anybody?'

'Peter Heneghan of Radio Merseyside wants you for interview.'

Then the cultured tones of John Mulholland's voice came crisply and clearly over the P.A. system:

'Happy Christmas and welcome to the CAFOD Christmas Run....'

By now there were hundreds of people, participants and spectators milling around the college grounds and the drive was clogged with cars.

'Would drivers please keep going - follow the signs to the car park. The drive must be kept clear.... And I repeat, welcome to this unique event organised to give us all the opportunity to share from our Christmas excess with the poorest of the poor.'

Peter Heneghan caught up with me;

'Can we find a quiet corner for an interview?'

'O.K. but let's make it snappy — time's getting on....'

'It looks like a successful event. Did you expect such a big response?'

'I should have done, but honestly, I didn't know what to expect.'

'Are the proceeds earmarked for anything specific?'

'Yes for CAFOD's relief and rehabilitation work in Ethiopia.'

'And how much do you hope to raise?'

'Anybody's guess, Peter — you know how generous the folks are in these parts.... Sorry I'll have to fly, somebody's calling me over there. I'll see you later.'

Bishop Tony Hitchen and Julian Filochonski at the Christmas Run

At one o'clock, Bishop Hitchen, standing on the stone wall by the college entrance, raised his right hand, and his voice:

'On your marks, get set....Go!'

Just over 400 runners, some seven-year-old, some 70, Mums and Dads, Grannies and Grandads, youth clubs, priests and nuns, St. Trinian's and Father Christmas too went charging down the drive, up the farm track, around the golf course, through the woods, around the playing fields.... and then started again for the second lap. And afterwards? .... exhaustion, aches and pains but no heart attacks, no blood spilt and the Red Cross had a quiet day.

I hurried to meet Bishop Hitchen who, as always, was beaming and in great good humour, and calling out *'Happy Christmas'* to anyone who caught his eye. Then turning to shake my hand warmly:

'Didn't I tell you that you'd pull it off? There must be thousands here.'

'Not quite, but there's a lot. We've given out four hundred numbers.'

'Well there must be twice as many spectators.'

Peter Callaghan joined us.

'Vin, sorry to interrupt but it's ten to one. They should be making their way to the start.'

'O.K. Peter, I'll get John to announce it.'

I drove home in moonlight through the same country lanes that I had travelled ten hours earlier, but in a much different frame of mind. I was happy and at peace with myself, enjoying that inner glow that comes with the knowledge and comfort of a job well done.

Pat Wilson

That first Run raised £7,000, and a year later, Christmas 1985, 800 runners brought in £12,000. Each successive year the numbers increased, the organisation improved — due especially to the appointment of Pat Wilson as my assistant. She brought great flair and professionalism to the task of promoting CAFOD in general and to the administration of the Run in particular. It soon became established as the biggest fund-raising event in CAFOD's calendar, attracting serious athletes as well as fun runners. The winner in 1990, Cades Cades, an Ethiopian and junior world half marathon champion, arrived unannounced at the last minute and then proceeded to break the course record in spite of having had to plough through a sea of mud. Julian Filochowski was a regular participant.

In 1993, to celebrate the 10th Run, three Masai tribesmen, our partners from Kenya, came to take part. That was a colourful spectacle as, in their traditional scarlet costume, they ascended the platform to greet the crowd, shouting, *'Happy Christmas and Merry New Year'*. Minutes later, in track suits, they led the field at the start on a carpet of snow followed by 1500 runners. It was a record turnout and the proceeds too hit an all time high — £32,000!

Two Bishops, Kevin O'Conner (left) and John Rawsthorne (right) supporting Vin in promoting the CAFOD Christmas Run

Vin with the 3 Maasai runners, Moronka, George and Kenny, for the Christmas Run

London

'If I were taken and pinioned for hours at a time in a shuddering, jerking box of steel and glass, lights flashed in my eyes, fumes blown up my nose and gas pumped into my lungs, if this were to be done by the Chinese, then I should be the subject of stern leaders in The Times and the righteous anger of the Daily Express. Yet I submit to this treatment of my own free will. I do it every week and it's called driving down to London.' — Alan Bennett

It was simply not my scene and it was truly a sense of vocation that took me to the capital. In February 1986, following the sacking of the Head of Appeals, I was prevailed upon to move to Head Office to fill the vacancy. But I was a family man with five children still going through various stages in their education, and to disrupt them with all the turbulence of moving house and school was unthinkable — so too was the suggestion of my working away from home on a permanent basis. Thus, I insisted that it was to be a temporary appointment, for though I had ample confidence and a wealth of experience, I had zero ambition — a wonderful combination that was not always understood.

Needless to say, I did not relish moving away from the comforts of home during the dark, damp days of winter, but there were one or two pluses, not least my being offered lodgings at St. Aloysius' by my good friend, Joe Ryan, the Parish Priest of that inner city parish close to Euston Station. Not all presbyteries, I am sure, would have been so welcoming, and the easy-going informality suited me down to the ground — not exactly an open house, but it oozed warmth and hospitality and there was always an interesting coming and going of visitors, to say nothing of the constant stream of 'down and outs' ringing the doorbell in hopeful anticipation of something to eat. As part of my induction to this interesting house, Joe instructed me on, and even demonstrated, the making of jam butties:

> 'Now follow this carefully. You take two slices from the packet; on one you put some margarine, on the other you put jam. Slap them together like that and that's what you give them — just that and no more when they come asking for a bite to eat.'

A day or two later I answered the door to a vagrant. He looked a pathetic sight, so being on my own in the place, I decided I would give him something a little more substantial — after all who would know? I served up two nice cheese butties. But the glow of self-righteousness that I nurtured and relished was soon to be extinguished in what had become the bizarre and daily routine — the rush and crush of London's underground where I, along with a seething mass of human flesh, was crammed into carriages to such an extent that any movement at all was verging on the miraculous, and breathing into each others' faces quite unavoidable. The return journey from Brixton was just a little better, but it was lightened with the eager anticipation of the evening meal and the 'good craic' (delightful conversation!) which always accompanied it. On this particular occasion, however, Joe was waiting for me:

> 'Vin, the number of callers at the door have increased today, nearly doubled in fact, and they all asked for you, the little fella with the Geordie accent. How do you account for that?'

> 'Joe, I haven't a clue.'

> 'If I believed that I'd believe anything. Now, listen, Vin, we can't feed the world at St.

Aloysius', and neither can we afford to buy cheese by the ton.' Then, with a grin he added, 'For your penance you have to eat the dinner cooked by me today. The housekeeper's on her day off.'

Joe, a quiet spoken Tipperary man of great good humour, kind and gentle by nature, was also a man of courage and resolve — even to the extent of confronting a Government Department. It happened like this. Pina, a young woman from the Philippines who came to this country to work in a London hotel on a four-year contract, soon became pregnant and subsequently gave birth to a son, Arman. The hotel would not offer her accommodation for herself and her baby and, unable to work, she found herself in breach of contract. Now classed as an illegal immigrant, she must leave the country, while Arman, a British citizen, could stay. In effect, she became a fugitive from the law, moving from pillar to post — one hostel to another — with neither counsellor nor professional advisor to help her to make application for legal status with the Immigration Office. When her plight came to Joe's notice she was already threatened with deportation. With little time for the paper work to be completed and find its way through the bureaucratic jungle, Joe acted quickly and decisively. He took advantage of the ancient law of sanctuary, whereby fugitives could be guaranteed protection by remaining within the confines of the church building. Thus, he brought Pina and her four-year-old son into St. Aloysius' — though in fact living accommodation was found for them alongside me in the adjoining presbytery and not, strictly speaking, within the church building itself. Joe negotiated on her behalf, arguing that it was unfair to deport a child who was a British subject. The negotiations lasted several weeks and during all this time, he manifested prudence as well as courage, for as an essential part of his strategy, he would not allow any publicity. This was not to become a public debate or a media circus. That might make it difficult for the government to give way. Joe's negotiations, then, were low key and his diplomacy behind the scenes. He sought only a compassionate outcome for Pina and Arman, and no kudos for himself whatsoever. That is exactly what he achieved.

The rain and grey mists of winter continued for another week or two then suddenly spring arrived early, and warm sunshine brought smiles to faces, cafes to pavements and daffodils to the parks, and very soon we forgot that it had ever rained. I took to strolling in the evening through the streets and squares and along the Embankment, and several times a week I jogged in Regents Park. Joe introduced me to an excellent Irish pub and I began to look a little more kindly on London, but nevertheless running for the 7.00 p.m. train to Liverpool on Friday remained the happiest task of the week.

The weekends flew and it seemed like no time at all before I was boarding the 6.20 a.m. on Monday so that I would be at my desk for 9.30 a.m. Head Office staff had increased, and office space, which for some time had been restrictive, was now considered to be grossly inadequate, and the powers that be were looking for a solution. By happy coincidence, Upholland College in Lancashire, which served the Northern Province as a seminary, was to close and a buyer was being sought. This would provide a superabundance of office space, conference facilities and even overnight accommodation for guests and overseas visitors, in a magnificent setting. It seemed to me to be a heaven-sent solution, so I floated the idea of moving lock, stock and barrel, pointing out that Manchester's International Airport was within thirty minutes drive and Wigan's main line rail station a mere four miles distance, and that Upholland is situated on the very edge of the motorway network.

I argued that with modern communications there was no need for a development agency to be located in the capital — after all there was a precedent with OXFAM. I was also convinced that if staff were given the opportunity to consider living in the countryside where the cost of housing was a fraction of that in London, where traffic congestion was more or less non-existent and where there were excellent schools close at hand, many would opt for the move north. It also seemed important to stress that such a move would have been a great prophetic gesture, for with much more expansion clearly on the horizon, it would bring jobs to an area of high unemployment. But the suggestion was not taken seriously and, subsequently, the existing building was extended on a very small site in Brixton and probably for a cost in excess of the asking price for the whole Upholland complex.

But in all other matters there was consultation in abundance.

'Meetings, meetings and more meetings — it's a wonder anything ever gets done.'

I think that I might have heard that said more than once, and I sometimes felt that I had entered a world where even the smallest of decisions loomed large and required approval by this committee or that and even an office junior, felt slighted if she had not been consulted. I was taken to task more than once for 'getting on with it' and not consulting. On one occasion I had produced a 'Thank You' card to send to donors, on which I thought that I had got everything right. The photograph was of a woman and she was black and she was a doctor and she was ministering to a sickly, malnourished man in Ethiopia. All the right messages — or so I thought. Surely this would satisfy the feminists and politically correct? But still I was brought to task. I had given it a caption, which simply read, 'Thank You'.

'We should not be saying, 'Thank you', for we are merely giving the poor what is theirs by right.'

....And so we had another meeting!

There were committees and working groups, departmental meetings, inter-departmental meetings, whole staff meetings and even one-to-one meetings. How I recall one such when I sat in a small office one warm and sunny afternoon listening to the office bore chuntering on and.... one of us fell asleep....

But best of all were 'away days' when a department or sometimes the whole staff would book a room in a school or a church hall. How many times have I sat in a circle with yawning colleagues at ten in the morning answering the question, 'What are your expectations for the day?' while an eager beaver 'facilitator' scribbled everyone's answers on to a flip chart. There followed a programme of brainstorming, role play exercises, poster games and all kinds of activities designed to help us achieve those expectations. At the end of the day, it was known to happen that, in order to affirm each other, a blank piece of A4 paper was pinned to everyone's back. We would then move around the room, from person to person, and with felt tip pen, write in a word or two, one of that person's qualities — definitely nothing negative! Each one could then, read : *'great guy, loyal, cheerful, great sense of humour, very efficient, generous, always happy, intelligent'* ....etc. That would put a spring in his step as he made for home!

.... Oops!.... her step.... or one's step as he/she made for home!

I recall the caretaker looking on while waiting to clear away. He pulled me to one side, shook his head in disbelief, then said:

'I was here at eight o' clock this morning getting things ready for you people. Since then I've cleaned the toilets, emptied the dustbins, weeded the drive, mowed the lawn and cleaned some windows. All for £140 a week. How much do you people get for playing bloody silly games?'

However, for most of the time, I felt a deep sense

Vin with Cafod's 'Top Brass' — from left to right: Bishop John Crowley, Cafod's Chairman; Archbishop Derek Worlock, Trustee; and Julian Filochowski, Director. Photo: Tom Murphy (Catholic Pictorial)

of privilege to be working at the Head Office of an official agency of the Church with some very fine people, but there were no saints on the staff and it would have been surprising if, within a large group, there were no tensions or clashes of personality. Feminism was strong and in some

quarters political correctness the order of the day. On one occasion when I referred to God as 'He', I was chastised that I could not even get the gender correct and, on another, I was to discover the ambiguity of the term 'partners', for my assumption was that it referred only to those people in the developing world with whom we were privileged to have a special relationship and through whom the funding of projects was facilitated, but I was to discover that sometimes it referred to the one with whom a member of staff was cohabiting — 'living over the brush', as we said up North; and of course; 'gay' no longer meant happy and carefree.

I also remember, in my naivete, being a little surprised at the number of colleagues who seemed to have no church allegiance. But on the whole, the nature of our work and the high sense of vocation that motivated some of the staff helped to promote a feeling of purpose and good will that made for a happy working atmosphere.

As one would expect, there were some strong personalities. The Projects Department was perceived to be the 'coal face', where all the important work was carried out, and where staff in daily contact with our overseas partners seemed constantly on the move, either returning from an overseas trip or planning the next. At certain times it amused me to observe them standing in the corridor on the occasion of a Management Committee Meeting, pale-faced and trembling nervously, waiting to be called to present projects for approval.

They were like school-leavers about to face their first interview, and yet they were intrepid travellers, sometimes journeying alone through some of the world's chief trouble spots. Off they took to far away places that so often hit the headlines because of some Emergency — drought, famine, hurricane, conflict or political unrest. CAFOD's important though less spectacular work of funding long-term development programmes did not so readily reach the headlines, thus the Education Department's role was to raise awareness of the causes of poverty and suffering in our world, and to remind Christians especially of their responsibility not only to share from their substance, but also to work for justice.

The Head of Development Education, and my close colleague in Head Office, was Brian Davies, an inspirational leader of a small team who, fired by the Gospel of social justice, gave great witness and ensured that the Church's social teaching and spirituality of justice was at the heart of all of CAFOD's work.

They were often referred to, good-naturedly, as the conscience of CAFOD, and that to a large extent was what they were. They produced excellent resources for schools and parishes, and Brian, something of a theologian, was in much demand to give talks and presentations at the highest level in Church circles. Thus, the Education Department, like the Projects Department, was perceived to have kudos that the Appeals Department did not enjoy.

My role, then, was basically to raise funds and to increase income, but I soon identified another priority — to raise self-esteem within a small group who, for one reason or another, felt despondent and under-valued. I concentrated, therefore, on raising spirits and creating a happy working atmosphere and I put a notice on the wall in bold lettering: '*Without Fundraising CAFOD Cannot Exist*'.

One of Brian's team gave special prophetic witness. These were turbulent times in the early Thatcher years, when the so-called nuclear deterrent was seen by many to be the greatest threat ever to the survival of the human race. Thousands took to the streets in peaceful protest. Some, regarding this as a faith issue, and wishing to give maximum publicity to the cause, decided to confront the government by peaceful, though unlawful means.

Pat Gaffney (not wearing her CAFOD hat) and a few of her friends, after prayerful preparation over several weeks, held a service on Ash Wednesday on the steps of the Ministry of Defence in Whitehall, during which they read well-chosen passages from scripture, sang hymns and prayed, then sprinkled the columns of the portico with ashes and their own blood and knelt in prayer in the entrance.

It was clear that the government had worked out a strategy of its own to deny publicity to such demonstrations — it was simply to ignore the protesters. After a while it became clear that they could not completely disregard a group of 'religious nuts' who defaced a government building and who were now persisting in prayer and obstructing the entrance.

Mr. Heseltine, the Secretary of State for Defence, was sent for, and clearly he too was at a loss, for it seemed that the last thing they wanted was the arrest of the demonstrators — that, they thought, would be playing into their hands. Eventually, however, the police came and they were arrested, but Pat and her friends had worked hard for the honour of spending a night in the cells. Their campaign lasted a few years, during which time Pat and her friends paid several visits to prison. Later, in order to pursue her vocation to promote peace and disarmament, she moved on and became General Secretary for Pax Christi.

As for me, my chief concern was the organising and co-ordinating of Family Fast Day twice a year throughout the parishes of England and Wales. This required, among other things, my liaising with the advertising agency and negotiating an imprimatur for all proposed promotion materials with the Director, the Education Department and others. Reaching a consensus was never easy, but I threw myself into my work and on the whole I enjoyed it.

At times I also found it exciting to be working at the nerve centre of CAFOD, where, among other things, I observed the gifted Director at close quarters - an efficient, and effective leader, but the recruitment of staff was certainly not one of his strengths, and finding a permanent Head of Appeals not one of his priorities. After three months, when my term of duty at Head Office should have come to an end, he had done nothing by way of recruiting a successor. I kept reminding him, but his response was always the same, to use all his powers of persuasion to get me to stay.

The salary was made to look very attractive, especially compared to the volunteer terms that I had while operating in the regions, but in spite of that, I remained unmoved and failed to be seduced by the charms and bright lights of London.

I wanted to be back home with my family where I belonged, so eventually, I spoke to Bishop Hitchen, then things started to move.

I was determined that, before I left Head Office, I would seek approval for the appointment of more Regional Organisers, since it was now acknowledged that the North-West pilot scheme had been a success. I presented a paper to the Management Committee, proposing the appointment of six Regional Organisers, which was approved.

During my last weeks at Head Office, Magdalena Gardener-Brown was appointed as Head of Appeals and Promotion — a delightful woman, who spoke in superlatives with a far-back accent and whose father had been a Director of Save The Children Fund.

Shortly afterwards, the second Regional Organiser was appointed, an ex-R.A.F. Group Captain, who had worked at the Ministry of Defence (perhaps he had stepped over Pat Gaffney on his way to work?) and whose brother was a bishop.

It was good to be home, not merely to enjoy domesticity but to fulfil my role once again as head of a family which was growing up all too quickly. Indolence, however, was not to have a look-in, for CAFOD was about to give birth to another heavy agenda - a programme of celebrations to mark its twenty-fifth anniversary.

Partners

*'We will go before God to be judged, and God will
ask us, "Where are your wounds?" And we will say,
"We have no wounds." And God will ask, "Was nothing
worth fighting for?"' — Rev. Alan Boesak, South Africa.*

In the middle of the road, in the very heart of Chaletanango, El-Salvador, stood a small, sturdy woman of about 40 years of age. The tall figure of the Commanding Officer stood over her with hands on hips and head lowered to meet her gaze. There was an air of determination in her bearing, and her head was raised in eye-ball-to-eye-ball confrontation. Her chubby arms gesticulated and her fingers stabbed the air as if to press home each point which she made with raised voice. This public remonstration attracted some attention from young soldiers, armed to the teeth, but keeping their distance. As for her companions looking on from the dubious safety of the truck, which had brought them to this hostile climate, they felt very uneasy as they surveyed the scene. The whole town was a seething mass of combat uniforms and military hardware.

Maria Julia was a Justice and Peace worker for the archdiocese of San Salvador and one of CAFOD's partners. She had driven us — that is, Austin Hughes, my close friend and CAFOD volunteer, Father Jim O'Keefe, member of CAFOD's Management Committee, Cathy Corcoran, Head of Projects, Clare Dixon, Latin America Projects Officer, and myself — from the capital on unkempt roads, treacherous for their state of disrepair but more so for military and terrorist activity. We were travelling with high hopes of reaching the border. There, we were to witness and speak to refugees returning to their homes after several years in virtual concentration camps in neighbouring Honduras. At each road block we were delayed while protracted negotiations and calls on field telephones eventually won permission for us to proceed, but only to the next checkpoint. Now it seemed we had reached the end of the road, for the military simply said,

'No, no further'.

But Maria Julia would not take 'no' for an answer, and we sat in the truck witnessing the animated discussion, while conversing with each other nervously — and in whispers too, for no good reason. Meanwhile our vehicle attracted much attention, but surely our pale faces were the main focus of interest. The haggling seemed to go on forever but in reality it was only a matter of minutes before she returned to her driving seat.

'O.K. we go!'

I was certain that we would be turning back, for he who was to be obeyed in that garrison town had seemed to match Maria Julia's determination with firm authority. However, her robust diplomacy had won the day, and we continued our journey to Guarjila near the Honduran border over terrain that would have been considered impassable in any developed country. There we met and spoke to refugees, who were already reclaiming their village and building temporary shelters on the sites of their demolished homes. Their small chapel, which had suffered severe damage from shellfire in past conflicts, had now been taken prisoner by nature, with trees and tropical plants filling its tiny nave and branches reaching to the sky through its broken roof. But a devout old man, cutting his way through the jungle which engulfed the church, made his way to the belfry. The bells had survived! He pulled and swung on the ropes with joyful abandon and their peal, which sent a squawking and fluttering of birds in all directions, also brought the whole community to the ruined chapel where they prayed and sang and brushed away their tears.

Our return journey was a hair-raising race against time to avoid travelling in darkness, and Maria Julia was again equal to the task — just another facet of her boldness. All day I had marvelled at her commitment and courage, whether she was arguing with the military, swinging the truck over perilous terrain or simply listening attentively to the cries of the poorest people in the world. At the end of the day when she might have taken her well-earned rest, she stayed with us and talked into the night. It was then that I realised that I

Vin with Maria Julia (centre) and a relief worker at the Salvador/Honduras border.

was in the company of someone very special indeed.

'Your visit to the returned refugees was very important — for you and for them. True solidarity! These poor people need to know that someone, somewhere cares about them. You see, to be poor doesn't just mean not to have money, it also means to be powerless — not to have friends with influence — nobody who can pull strings for them. The refugees you met today have nothing, not even documents, and in this society, that means they do not exist. The military stop them frequently and ask for their I.D. card. They have none, and no means of obtaining one, for the government will not issue them. Thus they do not exist and are vulnerable to all kinds of abuse, so I have produced official identity cards which include a photograph and states that they are members of the Archdiocese of San-Salvador, and they are signed by the Archbishop.

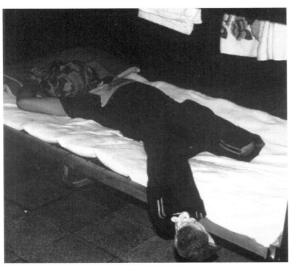

Amputee—child victim of a landmine

'Of course, my work is not only with refugees, much of my time is given to prison visits. Sometimes people die — or rather they are killed — in prison. I go to ask for the body, so that their family can arrange a Christian burial.'

'Surely this must put you in danger?'

Maria Julia took the question in her stride and in a matter of fact way, she replied:

'Yes, four of my predecessors were murdered, but I look at it like this: When Jesus died some of his disciples went to the authorities and asked for his body so that they might give him a dignified burial. In doing that, they identified themselves as his friends. I am simply doing the same.'

Monsignor Urioste

Partnership with the poor, we were constantly reminded, was a two-way process. After meeting Maria Julia it was easy to understand that we received at least as much from them as they did from us. Their faith, courage, life-style and example enriched our lives, but for me, it also meant that I was privileged to host in this country some very interesting people. One such person, also from El-Salvador, was Monsignor Urioste, personal friend of, and Vicar General to, Archbishop Romero. I organised his programme of press and radio interviews and his speaking engagements during his brief visit to the North-West of England. There were in Liverpool, at this time, Central America Solidarity Groups, so already there was some awareness of the oppression of the poor and repression by the military, which served an extreme right-wing

Oscar Arnulfo Romero, Archbishop of San Salvador

of human rights and the sinful structures in society which caused so much misery to the vast majority of his people. He was assassinated while celebrating Mass. Prophetically, two weeks before his death, he said in an interview:

> 'I am bound, as a pastor, by a divine command to give my life for those whom I love, and that is all Salvadoreans, even those who are going to kill me .... Can you tell them, if they succeed in killing me, that I pardon and bless those who do it. But I wish that they could realise that they are wasting their time. A bishop may die, but the Church of God, which is the people, will never die.'

I visited the scene of his martyrdom, the convent chapel of a cancer hospital on the outskirts of San Salvador, where he was pumped with bullets as he celebrated Mass. The simple plaque on the front of the altar reads:

> 'Greater love hath no man than he lays down his life for his friends.'

government, in that troubled country. There was also devotion, especially among justice and peace activists, to Archbishop Romero, whom they had already canonised by popular acclaim. He was their hero, saint and martyr.

Like so many prophets before him, Monsenor, as he was affectionately called by his people, suffered a violent death for condemning the abuse

The place of his martyrdom - now a shrine

Once again, I knew that I was on holy ground.

Nobody had known the Archbishop better than Monsignor Urioste, and his visit to Liverpool intensified popular devotion. But there is always one dissenting voice, and I recall when he spoke to an audience of priests, one of them, a well known conservative, posed the question that perhaps the Archbishop had been manipulated. The Monsignor paused thoughtfully, and then quietly and gently recounted an incident when a Government Minister called to see the Archbishop:

'I went to his room to tell him that his visitor had arrived, but he was not there. I looked in other rooms, but could not find him. I searched everywhere and then finally I looked in the chapel. There he was on his knees before the Blessed Sacrament. Yes, I think he was being manipulated.'

PHILIPPINES

There was no moon, no stars, no lights. It was black dark. I had found four bamboo walls with a threadbare roof, deserted. There was a bed of sorts — a thin mattress on slats. I had walked over mountains in Zamboanga del Sur on the island of Mindanao, Philippines in the intense heat of the afternoon sun, and in the cool of the evening, I had slaked my thirst and had eaten. To lie down wherever, was blessedness beyond words, for even on my feet I had been in a semi-comatose state, and now I was horizontal and drifting slowly but ever surely into oblivion. Suddenly I was shaken with a rattle of gunfire, shouting, a

Karl Gaspar, inspirational leader of the poor

sweeping of searchlights and the wail of a siren. More gunfire, more shouting, then silence....

All was quiet now. I lay awake and prayed, then after a minute or two, the faint sound of footsteps broke the silence — they were approaching, getting louder.... closer. I held my breath. Then the door kicked open and a voice called,

'Vin, it's me, Karl. I've come to sleep here beside you because of the military activity. I thought you might be nervous.'

A Farmer struggling for survival in Mindanao

It took a while for me to regain the blissful state of somnolence of just a few minutes ago, and I lay awake contemplating the courage of Karl, who had taken his own life in his hands for my safety and peace of mind.

Karl Gaspar is a CAFOD partner. He was also a Church Worker during the vicious Marcos dictatorship and, because of his commitment to justice, served a prison sentence, which he embraced as a period for reflection. On his release he joined the Redemptorist Order as a lay brother. He now leads a mission team, helping to form Basic Christian Communities, and it was my privilege to walk with him into the remote areas of the Philippines when, in 1990, I made a return visit, not strictly on CAFOD business this time, but 'under my own steam'.

Terrorists taking refuge in the hills, from time to time emerge to conduct an assault against the military. Simply being there can be perilous because of night skirmishes and the constant danger of being caught in crossfire. The company one keeps can add to the danger.

'What does your wife think about your coming here to walk with me on the Malindang mountain range, the most notable hot-spot for terrorist activity?'

'The truth is, Karl, she doesn't really know. Come to think of it, neither did I till I got here.'

We stayed overnight with farmers who told us their stories of constant harassment by the military, who, suspecting that they may be harbouring, or at least feeding, terrorists, will from time to time put their homes to the torch and the poor farmers and their families are forced to flee for their lives. But since they have nowhere else to go on a permanent basis, when the dust settles they return to pick up the pieces and start again. These are Karl's people.

'My vocation is to be a brother.... sometimes this causes confusion, because the popular conception is that you are either a priest or layman.... But I look at it positively.... I have a vocation - to be of service to the poor.'

Karl has walked with me in this country too, visiting parishes in England and Wales where his talks and other presentations have enlightened and entertained, for he is a gifted speaker, writer and musician. In Liverpool I took him to see the Cathedrals, but his priority was to make a pilgrimage to the shrine of The Beatles — a trip down memory lane — where he relived some of the joy and excitement of his student days in his home town, Davao City, Philippines.

Smokey Mountain

While in Manila, I called into NASSA (no, not the space agency) — National Secretariat For Social Action - CAFOD's partner agency in the Philippines. There, I renewed acquaintance with Sister Evelyn of the Good Shepherd Congregation, a kind of 'Jim'll fix it' character, who had hosted my first visit to

Manila's slums in 1984, and who, I felt sure, would help me to visit Smokey Mountain, where masses of people scratch for a living amidst squalor and filth on that infamous rubbish dump.

I arrived at Smokey Mountain at 3.00 p.m. What a shock! I thought that I had seen everything in terms of human degradation, but this is the worst place on earth. It really is everything that people say it is — a vast filthy mountain of rotting rubbish of every kind, where thousands of families live, scavenging through garbage and excrement. The rotting rubbish produces methane gas which bursts into flames by spontaneous combustion, producing smoke that chokes and fumes that poison. Little wonder that life expectancy is very low and infant mortality sky-high. And the

Children of Smokey Mountain

survivors? How can they be anything other than dirty, undernourished carriers of disease? Grandparents, mothers, fathers and children labour every day looking for something that might bring a few pesos. Some, specialising in tin, collect cans in huge baskets, which they carry on their backs, others gather plastic only, while some seem to go for anything, rubber, plastic, tin or whatever — and sometimes they even find something to eat! Their homes, surrounded in a sea of putrefaction, are made from refuse — so too are the shops, cafes and a chapel — and yet they make attempts to beautify them with flowers. There was a gentleness too that seemed out of place in such a hell-hole. When I tentatively produced a camera, they did not object — on the contrary they co-operated and brought their children to be included in the picture. Perhaps my visit broke the monotony — but who knows what they made of me? It was an unbelievable experience.

ETHIOPIA

The war that had raged in Ethiopia for thirty years was over when I visited in 1992. There had been a pleasant take-over of the capital, Addis Ababa, by the Ethiopia Peoples' Revolutionary Democratic Front (EPRDF), and democracy was in place. No longer was food stored merely to service the war, and the head of state, President Meles Zenaiwi, had promised free elections within two years. To one inexperienced traveller in Africa making his first visit to Ethiopia, it appeared that there was a good feeling abroad, but Brother Gus

Market in Wallaito Soddo — Ethiopia

O'Keefe of the Holy Spirit Congregation, and CAFOD's chief partner, reminded me (if I needed reminding) that there were still many problems:

'For one, there are too many guns around. When Mengistu fled the country and found sanctuary in Zimbabwe, his soldiers also took flight and many of them sold their weapons to buy food, while others simply became bandits, making the highways, in the more remote areas, especially hazardous for travellers. That is why I have given you a driver who is also your bodyguard. You are in very safe hands.'

Alemayo was a tall, thick-set man in his fifties, with full moustache and dressed western style with collar and tie and a trilby worn deep into his brow. He spoke fluent English with an air of authority and was not given to small talk. He did not smile much either, but nevertheless, was generally of a pleasant disposition.

'Tomorrow we leave early — eight o' clock sharp, for we must arrive by mid-afternoon. It's very dangerous to be travelling later in the day.'

On the dusty roads, at times hardly discernible through semi-desert, Alemayo exuded quiet confidence, negotiating the many pot-holes with ease. We were travelling by landrover two hundred miles through a landscape deforested and parched but which, in places, was surprisingly varied and occasionally breath-taking in its beauty, to Wallaito Soddo in the south, where I was to be hosted by the Daughters of Charity. The predominant feature for most of the journey was the vast

Ethiopian shepherd boy

number of goats and cattle being led by malnourished children in search of water and pasture, but as we approached our journey's end, the parched landscape gradually gave way to grassland and cultivated fields. There were trees and blossoms too, and the whole panorama was transformed into one of verdant beauty.

Wallaito Soddo was a town of bustling activity with a large and fascinating market, where a jumble of live poultry and animals, vegetables, clothes, household goods, herbs and tobacco were bought and sold and where pipe-smoking women squatted in the dust selling their wares. Though fascinating, we gave it only a few minutes

Beauty and dignity — an Ethiopian Mother and child

of our time, for I was more than ready for refreshment and rest.

A tug at the convent bell brought a gaggle of nuns to the door.

'Hello, you must be Vin.... and General!.... Oh this is a surprise.'

'General' was the title the sisters bestowed on my bodyguard-cum-chauffeur, and they explained to me that during the reign of Haile Selassie,

'The 'General' was Chief of Police for the whole of Ethiopia. After the revolution, he served many years in prison. And now, the war over, he works for the Church.'

It was obvious that they were very proud of the General, and they bubbled with excitement, each one trying to get a word in.

'How lovely to see you both.'

'Did you have a good journey?'

'Come this way. We have drinks ready for you. You must be dropping.'

We sat in a comfortable lounge under electric fans and slaked our thirst.

'No incidents on the way?'

'No, we left early and only stopped once, and that was for lunch.'

'Where did you stop?'

'Sheshamane.'

I thought I spotted the sisters exchanging glances and perhaps a few raised eyebrows at this last piece of news, but we were distracted when an older sister appeared on the scene.

'Vin, you were a friend of my brother, Peter.'

'Was I?.... Not Peter Heery? .... I don't believe it!.... Goodness gracious, what a coincidence.'

Peter was my closest friend, who had died of cancer just a few months previously. I knew that his sister, Jane, was a nun working somewhere in Africa, but I was astounded to discover that I had stumbled across her on my second day in Ethiopia. It was also for me a most fortunate coincidence that she was also a nursing sister, for the mystery of the raised eyebrows at the mention of Sheshamane was to be revealed next day. The whole community was waiting for it to happen, and it did — the most violent attack of food poisoning imaginable! I was subjected to 24 hours of intensive care and oral rehydration under the watchful gaze of sister Jane.

The convent was principally a Montessori College of Education with a Teacher Training Programme. There was also a Women's Co-operative — an income-generating project, but the most moving of all was the Emergency Feeding Programme — the very poorest of the poor knew where to go when they were hungry, for relief work was not new to the sisters. They had been at the very centre of the worst-affected part of Ethiopia during the great famine of 1984-85.

The memory I shall cherish of the Daughters of Charity at Wallaito Soddo was their commitment, compassion, efficiency and professionalism, but more — they were such fun to be with, and when we left at dawn on our return journey to Addis Ababa, the whole community (all six of them) were there to give us a joyful send-off.

We had travelled for about an hour on the silent road through wide open countryside with only an occasional herdsman to greet us with raised hand and a smile. The sun shone red and the sand glowed pink all around. Then in the distance I saw, silhouetted against the early morning sky, the black shapes of men busily engaged in some activity that turned my stomach. I looked to Alemayo, but his face, impassive, betrayed no emotion and he stared ahead without uttering a word. As we drew close I could see that they had placed rocks across the road — quite obviously the beginnings of a road block. There were four, each holding a spear in one hand, and with the other, waving us to stop. Alemayo, still impassive, slowed down and as they approached, he slipped into a low gear then revved the engine, we jerked forward, and he accelerated. There was a scattering of potential assailants and we crashed over the smaller rocks. The landrover bumped and leaped and jerked, cleared the would-be obstruction, while at least one spear bounced off the rear door, and then we zoomed hell for leather over ruts and ridges and potholes for about a mile. It was then that Alemayo broke his silence:

'A few minutes later and they would have finished that wall.'

It could so easily have been a different story.

KENYA

Of all the situations I had ever been in, surely this was the most extraordinary. I was sitting in the back of a landrover being driven through a jungle in Masai Land, Kenya, when a family of giraffes nonchalantly crossed our path, and similarly, a little later, we gave way to twenty or more ostriches who strolled past and on reaching a clearing, formed a circle and did a dance, and then all manner of creatures kept turning up — elephants, monkeys, gazelles, zebras, and birds of every size and colour.

Of course, I had expected to see wild animals, but not so many, so frequently, at such close quarters — and in such variety! These images, I had thought, belonged to the world of television and cinema and to a large extent were simply the products of special effects and editing. I had reservations about their authenticity as portrayed on the silver screen.

The real thing, I thought, would surely be less spectacular — and yet here I was captivated by the reality — infinitely more colourful, prolific and beautiful than the wit of man could ever reproduce. It was simply enchanting.

I was being hosted by our partner, Kenny Matampash, and first stop was a remote village, the enkang, in the heart of the jungle, where I was to spend the night and enjoy Masai hospitality. I declined the invitation to select the goat that was to be roasted in my honour, but there was no escaping my witnessing its being choked to death in the traditional manner. The drinking of its warm blood was more than I could stomach and I called upon the diplomacy of Kenny to extricate me from what might have become an embarrassing moment.

The lighting of the fire intrigued me, and I was taken back to my days as a boy scout when I tried for hours on end to produce flames by rubbing two sticks together, without ever achieving even the faintest glimmer of a spark. The Maasai warriors on the other hand had a blaze going within minutes and soon after I was being force-fed chunks of roasted flesh — in the nicest possible way — though it was tough and bland. Then out of the jungle came the monkeys to join the barbecue: I had never known till then that they were carnivores. The feast continued until sundown when the night sky and sounds of crickets and many other creatures captured my interest. I was comforted to see bushes, with huge thorns like darning needles, forming a protective barrier against wild animals - lions, leopards, hyenas and jackals.

I then turned in for the night in a mud hut donated by Kenny's sister where, before I dropped off to sleep soundly in pitch blackness on a lion's skin, I pondered the exceptional happenings of the day and my thoughts inevitably transported me once again to home, so far removed from everything around me.

There is no doubt that there had been more memorable days and countless happier days too, especially in the context of family. First there was our honeymoon in County Cork and then, as the years went by, celebrating the birth of each of our five children and the joy of Christmases and camping holidays — surely all more happy and more blessed than anything I could have hoped for. But there is equally no doubt that the most extraordinary day of my life was the one that I had just spent in the heart of a Kenyan jungle.

Inside, my mud hut was dark and cool and free from mosquitoes and flies but a

The barbecue - Maasai style

million other insects shared my abode — they lived inside the cow dung which plastered the walls — and their singing was a lullaby which sent me swiftly to sleep. At daybreak I learned that by poking a finger through the wall at a certain point, a sunray would provide sufficient light by which to dress, though the truth is I slept fully clothed. When I emerged, I was greeted with the sights and sounds of nature blending with human activity — a four-or-five-year-old girl with beaker in hand was pulling at a goat's udders to obtain her breakfast milk, and two older boys were

Maasai herdsmen

delicately performing the operation to extract blood from the vein in a cow's neck. Others were already on their way walking with livestock, for the Maasai are nomads, and pastoralists and must be always on the move, looking for water and pasture for their animals. Their lives are devoted to the care of their cattle — the source of their nourishment in both milk and blood and the greeting a Maasai gives to his friend when they meet along the path of the savannah, '*I hope your cows are well*', reflects the first concern of their lives.

However, I had not come simply to be fascinated by their culture and customs. I had come to take photographs and video footage of the Development Programme — community based projects in health, water and sanitation and animal

Kenny Matampash, CAFOD's partner—Kenya

welfare. My guide and companion was Kenny Matampash, one of the few Masai who have had a western-style education.

'It was during colonial times, when I was about eight years of age, a British Officer came to our village and lined up all the boys. He then measured their height in a cursory manner — those who stood taller than his rifle were dismissed, those shorter were selected for boarding school. My family were heartbroken; they all wept. My mother thought that she had lost her son, and that I would be deprived of my birthright, which is the traditional education and formation of the Masai. I would miss out on the traditions of the fathers too — songs, dances and warfare. I would not become a defender of their land and cattle.'

His mother need not have worried, for though her son progressed to higher education, and has of course, in many ways become westernised, he has not forsaken his roots and, as a development worker, is often called upon to defend the land rights of his people, not with violence, but in the courts of law. He travels widely, but keeps a base in his home village close to his family.

'How old are you, Kenny?'

'I don't know. That's not important, but it is important to know who I am. I am forever a Maasai.'

When my work for CAFOD was complete I stayed on for a holiday in that fascinating country and was joined by Gill. Kenny took time off too and insisted on hosting our holiday. He and two of his Maasai friends George and Moronka, were our Guardian Angels through the Amboseli Safari Park on our way to Loitokitok where Father John Cooper of the diocese of Hexham and Newcastle was Parish Priest and where we stayed at the mission in a chalet at the foot of Kilimanjaro, Africa's highest mountain. By now, my eyes were becoming accustomed to paradise rediscovered, but as for Gill, she was still enchanted and intoxicated by the splendour. The exquisite Thompson gazelles in their thousands were her favourites, but she 'oohed and aahed' constantly at zebras, giraffes,

The Chalet where Gill and Vin stayed. Kilimanjaro, Africa's highest mountain in the background.

Gill making friends with a young Maasai mother.

that, we were more than ever mesmerised by the sheer quantity of the riches of Kenya. Most, if not all, of the mammals native to East Africa, and an immense variety of birds, are there to be enjoyed. The challenge is to hunt and photograph the big five — elephant, buffalo, lion, leopard and rhino — within a day. We managed only four — the rhino being the elusive one — and drove very close to a family of lions who were making short work of a zebra that was still steaming from the chase.

Though all of the big five are dangerous and to be treated with the greatest of respect, our Maasai

leopards and lions and the superabundance of beasts and birds of every colour and size. We walked on the lower slopes of snow-capped Kilimanjaro escorted by Bernard Leiyian, a Church Worker and Masai elder, whose gentle courtesy remains vivid in our memory, so too the wrinkled and barefoot elder, whose role was gatekeeper to the mission compound. His only English was, *'no problem'*. Each morning I greeted him, *'Good morning'*, and his unfailing reply was, *'No problem!'*

We travelled to the Maasai Mara still accompanied by Kenny, George and Moronka. In one way it could be described as more of the same, but it was so much more of the same — by far the biggest and best Game Park in Kenya —

'The Lion's share'

hosts, while vigilant for our safety, had no compunction about approaching the big five from the safe confines of the landrover — with the exception of one.

> 'Inside our car, the only one to be afraid of is a charging elephant. He could overturn even a big vehicle.'

Needless to say we kept our distance.

We moved on to Nanyuki where Kenny, George and Moronka said an emotional but cheerful goodbye, then passed us on to the warm hospitality of the Consolata Fathers with whom we stayed for the final few days. We took advantage of the situation and climbed Mount Kenya to a height of 14,200ft. What an experience! Walking in high altitude for the first time in our lives was like climbing a lakeland fell while suffering from a heavy dose of flu, taking ten paces then resting before attempting another ten, then resting again and so on. How thankful we were at dusk to arrive at McKinder's Camp, a cluster of huts in an ice field — and on the equator too! The nauseous feeling persisted, and though food was on offer, we declined and took to the wooden slatted bunks wrapped in sleeping bags provided by porters, where we slept fitfully in the thin atmosphere. The next day our recovery rate was rapid, in proportion to the rate of our descent.

Our Kenya adventure was at an end and the next day we made our way to Nairobi Airport with mixed feelings, for while we looked forward to our homecoming, we also felt a little sad to be leaving a country bathed in a perfect climate and so full of beauty and fascination. As we struggled with our luggage to the departure desk, three pairs of hands relieved us of our burdens — it was Kenny, George and Moronka. They had come with gifts to say goodbye.

Proclaim Jubilee

In 1987, CAFOD marked its twenty-fifth birthday, by proclaiming a Jubilee — a whole year of celebrating our partnership with the poor, but not mere merrymaking and junketing by any means. It was a time of deep reflection for the whole of CAFOD's constituency and an occasion to campaign for, and to honour, the poor and oppressed in the Third World. Focusing on the biblical notion of Jubilee when, in Old Testament times, every fifty years on the day of Atonement, a ram's horn (shofar) was blown to signal a new beginning. This was to be a time of liberating freedom for all the people when debts were to be forgiven, land was to be restored for the use and benefit of all and slaves set free.

On a stormy winter's evening in early January in Liverpool's Metropolitan Cathedral, Rabbi Kay, of Southport synagogue, gave a blast from the shofar to herald the opening of our Jubilee year. This was followed by an impressive procession to the sanctuary, where Archbishop Worlock, attended by many priests, concelebrated Mass. During the months that followed there were many joyous occasions for the whole of CAFOD, and for me, though hard at work, every day was a Jubilee and I awoke each morning with a smile on my face.

Vin introducing Cardinal Arns from Brazil, in Salford Cathedral

Paul V1 of happy memory, whose Encyclical Letter, Populorum Progressio was the inspiration and manifesto of CAFOD. Cardinal Arns of Brazil gave the first of these lectures in London, but also visited the North-West of England where he spoke to the faithful in Salford Cathedral. His whole address on the Jubilee theme was inspirational but, focusing especially on international debt, his closing remarks brought a packed congregation to its feet to deliver resounding applause;

'This is certainly a question of world peace and of world democracy. But it is, above all, an ethical question of justice in international relationships.

For example, if this debt is paid in full at high interest rates, many in the Third World will die or have their health seriously damaged.

But if we don't pay back these high interest charges no one is going to die in the United States, Germany, France or Britain.... Our common task, then, is to fulfil the ideal of the Jubilee year; announcing Good News to the poor.'

These were busy as well as happy times. Events and conferences were superimposed on an already packed agenda but 'keeping my eye on the ball', the main thrust of my work continued to be the setting up of support groups in parishes throughout the North-West of England, and I was privileged to be working with some very good people, who, looking at the wider world through the eyes of faith, took an option for the poor. It was my privilege to introduce to them partners from the developing world who came to join the celebrations, tell their stories, and to share with us their hopes and dreams.

An annual lecture was instituted in honour of Pope

But our task was also to announce good news from the poor, for as our friends and visitors constantly reminded us, the poor have much to share with us — not least the Kingdom of Heaven — and sometimes they challenge our lifestyle too.

Bernard Guri from Ghana hangs his scarf on the Shankley Gate at Anfield at the time of the Hillsborough disaster

Bernard Guri came from Ghana. Speaking on environmental issues, he compared our throw-away society with the other world of the poor where he came from.

He recalled his first experience of supermarket superabundance and how he was given two plastic carrier bags, which he put under his bed ready for the next shopping trip. But the next time, he was quite surprised to be given another two and subsequently two more. After a while he had quite a stockpile under his bed.

> 'This is the way you live,' he said. 'We use things until they are destroyed. We carry water in old cans, and if they puncture, we repair them.'

He recalled how on a rubbish tip in this country he saw much that people in Africa would use to furnish their homes:

> 'You have created advertisements to tempt yourselves to buy things you don't need — then you throw away good things to make room for them. We in the Third World are destroying our environment cutting wood for fuel. Soon there will be no trees left — just desert in many countries. The environment is a luxury only those with plenty have time to worry about. You eat chocolate biscuits and you haven't even seen a cocoa tree. We pick cocoa beans and have never tasted chocolate. I tell you, there is only one way to save the environment — poverty must be eliminated. How? You must have less. We must have more.'

One of our regular visitors was Joseph Donders, affectionately known as Sjef, a Dutchman who had worked for many years as a missionary priest in Africa and was also a highly respected theologian. He was surely one of the most intelligent people it has been my privilege to host — but also one of the most lovable and welcome of guests, and very much one of the family. His gentle and joyful personality oozes an irresistible charm that captures friendship wherever he goes, and the mere mention of his name can warm the heart and give birth to a smile. He is a world traveller, in constant demand for his gifts as an inspirational speaker and for his scriptural insights, and at his best when delivering a radical message to challenge even the most conservative of minds without raising the temperature or increasing the pulse rate within his audience. It was from Sjef more than any other person that I learnt the lesson — it is not what you say, but how you say it.

I remember one occasion very well, when Sjef was asked to address a group of middle-class Christians, well known for their right-of-centre views and fundamentalist approach to scripture.

Sjef with Gill walking in the Lake District at Grasmere.

Sjef decided to gently disturb them and he took for his text the feeding of the hungry from John's Gospel in the sixth chapter. His very good English spoken with a most attractive Dutch accent of course helped, but when he almost acted out each part as he retold the story with great good humour and childlike enthusiasm, he won his audience completely. It is impossible to do justice in the retelling, but the gist went something like this;

> 'In this story there are some very interesting points to consider: It was evening when the disciples confronted Jesus saying, "Look these people are hungry". Jesus' reply may seem very strange, "Give them something to eat". How on earth were they expected to do that? According to John a little boy offered some bread and some fish. Jesus took it and then things started to happen and everybody ate their fill. There was even plenty left over.

'Now perhaps you believe, like most people, that the loaves and fishes, which the boy gave so generously, were miraculously multiplied — that Jesus took some bread and fish in his hands and gave it to someone. Then another piece of fish and bread appeared in his hand. And that this happened again and again. Others believe another type of miracle took place.

> First of all, let us consider the boy. Does it not seem strange that a small boy still had some food left so late in the day? Young boys usually eat their sandwiches sooner rather than later! If he had something left, is it possible that the adults also had some food hidden away in their pockets? Perhaps they were reluctant to produce it in case they had to share? Did Jesus and the little boy change all that? When the people saw them break the bread and give to others, perhaps

that is when they produced their food and the sharing began.

'The first interpretation is where the bread and fish are multiplied, the second is where the hearts of people are broken open to each other. There was enough food there all the time. The miracle was a miracle of sharing. Is not this the kind of miracle that our world needs today?

'There is enough food in the world for every child, woman and man to have three good meals every day with plenty left over. Yet nearly one thousand million people will go to bed hungry tonight.'

A tiny miracle took place in that church hall that night too, for during his talk there were nods and smiles of agreement and when he finished there was a thoughtful silence followed by suggestions, recommendations and finally resolutions passed as to how that small middle-class, comfortably conservative community might share more generously with the poor.

"When I give food to the poor they call me a Saint. When I ask why the poor have no food, they call me a Communist."
So said Bishop Helder Camara from Brazil.

(left) Bishop Helder Camara on a visit to this country, on the arm of Bishop Tony Hitchen of Liverpool. (They are both deceased).

Also pictured, Jeffrey Pereira of Bangladesh with the author.

Photo: Carlos Reyes

Negros

*'This is what Yahweh asks of you, only this,
to act justly, to love tenderly, and to walk
humbly with your God.'* — Micah chapter 6.

Some of the welcoming party

Not all of my visits to the Philippines were on CAFOD business. In 1992 I took off under my own steam and travelled widely, visiting several islands and deepening my attachment for that beautiful country and its people. Perhaps the poorest of these islands is Negros, which now has a special place in my affection.

Winston Tanaman was my facilitator, interpreter

and guardian angel. A young man of 30 years, quiet, gentle but incredibly brave, he was a human rights worker, an artist, writer and photo-journalist, who took me into some of the remote areas where extremist groups, fanatically opposed to Basic Christian Communities, ran amok perpetrating all kinds of mindless violence and murder on innocent families. Through Winston I was able to talk to some of the victims of human rights abuse. One such person was Maria Fe Canlum.

In a disused Youth Centre which served as a sanctuary for evacuees I spoke to her and her

Murdered family victims of fanatical group

Photo: Winston Tanaman

Maria Fe Canlum   Photo: Winston Tanaman

children — just one of the many families that had fled from their homes in Southern Negros because of the brutality inflicted on them by fanatical vigilante groups, who suspected them of being sympathisers of the communist guerrillas. They were nothing of the kind, but simply poor, hardworking farmers and members of Basic Christian Communities. Maria Fe was the mother of twelve children. Tears streamed down her cheeks as she relived the day when members of the group known as the Greenans came to their farm to question her about her husband who at the time was working in the fields. When they left she became worried about her husband's safety, so in the late afternoon, when he had not returned, she went with her children to look for him. They found his headless body with many stab wounds. Afraid to return to their home in case they too might be killed, Maria fled with her children to the hills, where for a week they lived on roots and berries. They became severely malnourished, so Maria Fe went back to her home where she knew a little money was hidden. With this, to buy food on the way, she set out with her children to walk 200 kilometres to the capital, Bacolod, where she had heard that Bishop Fortich gave sanctuary and support to the poor, especially evacuees. They walked for a week, with Maria carrying her baby all the way.

At the evacuation centre, which resembled a run-down campsite with few facilities, life was very hard. The refugees lacked food, sleeping mats, clothes and medicines. The local Basic Christian Community came to share what little they had, but that was indeed very little, for on the island of Negros, there was, and still is, extreme poverty and widespread malnutrition. Living almost entirely on a diet of rice, the children were lethargic at their best and frequently sick. The infant mortality rate was very high.

> 'Life is very hard, but worst of all for a mother is to listen to her sick child crying in the night and knowing there is simply nothing she can do.'

It was my privilege to travel widely with Winston visiting sugar plantations and staying in the homes of the exploited poor. As we journeyed through this beautiful but troubled island, I spent a little time with Columban priests. I was greatly impressed, not so much by their theological and political wisdom, though they had both in great measure, but by their warmth and compassion for the poor whom they served.

In La Carlota City we received a tremendous welcome from the parishioners of Our Lady Queen Of Peace and their amazing parish priest, Father Greg Patino, who had more than fifty emergency feeding centres for children to his credit and several income-generating projects for urban poor and sugar workers. His was a familiar story of harassment and death threats by those who opposed his commitment to the cause of social justice and human liberation, seeing it not as devotion to his Christian faith, which it was, but as an expression of communism, which it most certainly was not. A tiny man, standing a mere

Father Greg Patino

Estrella Sunggay watches over her son having a lunch of wheat.   Photo: Winston Tanaman

five feet tall, with the heart of a lion, Father Greg stood his ground and continued to serve his flock steadfastly.

Yet another blessing was to receive the warm hospitality of Bishop Fortich when he welcomed me into his home. His Pastoral Letter defending the rights of the poorest and most exploited workers in the sugar industry had brought about bitter opposition from the rich and powerful landowners.

> 'Beloved brethren, the position and appeals which I have here stated may sound revolutionary to some. It is not so; I merely reiterate the clear teaching of the Church and reflect the expectation and the right of every man and woman in my diocese to a better life.'

His option for the poor was much too challenging for some of his former friends who now had become his bitterest enemies. He beamed as he told me that he was even more privileged to be identified more closely with the poor when his opponents completely destroyed the historic Bishop's Palace by fire. The walls of his present, more modest home, had been strafed by bullets during the several attempts on his life. A few weeks before my visit, a grenade was hurled through his window — yet another narrow escape. When President Aquino telephoned him to offer sympathy, he remarked, *'I am in good shape and whoever did it, I have already forgiven.'*

The Church in Negros is not only a Church of the poor, it is a Church which is poor, so it is not surprising that Winston, a highly professional person, and my friend and companion, who worked for the diocese of Bacolod, should have a very frugal lifestyle. Nor is it too surprising that

Father Philip Inch, Liverpool Youth Chaplain, making friends with the help of lollipops on the island of Negros

in a country where more than 90 per cent of its people are denied such basic rights as adequate diet, healthcare and housing, he himself, should succumb to tuberculosis — very much the disease of the poor. He wrote to me from his sick bed,

> 'I still hope that I will recover and I know that God is beside me and still has a loving mission for me to fulfil. I want to continue my work with God's people.'

Winston died aged 34 years on May 19th 1995.

The Philippines hosted World Youth Day in 1995 and the Pope went to join in the celebrations. So too did a group of young people from Liverpool accompanied by Bishop John Rawsthorne and Youth Chaplain Father Philip Inch.

From the beginning of their preparations it was thought that travelling to the ends of the earth to visit a developing country would also present an opportunity for the group to meet the people at grass roots level and share something of their way of life, taste their culture, learn something about their problems and how they and the Church in the Philippines were facing up to these problems.

Bishop John Rawsthorne visits a family — the poorest of the poor

It was my privilege to lead them on an Exposure Programme to the island of Negros.

From the moment we set foot on the island, we experienced hospitality beyond our wildest dreams. At the airport the welcoming party of some thirty or forty people was assembled with huge banners, garlands were placed around our necks and we received the warmest of welcomes.

From then on, at every port of call, the reception and cordiality intensified, and at one parish it seemed like the whole town had turned out to give an overwhelming greeting. But even more moving, for the Liverpool lads, were their experiences of living with the poorest of the poor in Basic Christian Communities, sleeping on the floor of their bamboo homes, listening to their stories of struggle and their aspirations for justice based on a deep faith and nourished by the Gospel.

These young people from opposite ends of the earth celebrated, sang, laughed and sometimes wept together. The Filipinos gave several dramatic performances - one in particular stands out when they enacted how, as a community, they worked for justice and as a consequence suffered harassment and even murder. Bishop Rawsthorne, speaking afterwards, said,

> 'Never at any time in any place can I remember being so moved by a performance.'

At the blessing of a small irrigation project, one of the community leaders made a brief, emotional speech, his voice breaking as the tears flowed freely down his cheeks. After all their struggles and hard work they were blessed with God's precious gift of water for their crops — and a bishop had come all the way from England to bless their efforts!

Nobbled

'Don't stop doing things because you're growing old,
or you'll grow old because you stop doing things.'

By now I was forced to take some time off — Gill saw to that. We would escape for a long weekend to our caravan on West Shield Hill, or in high summer travel further afield to the magnificent Western Highlands and Islands of Scotland, where we learned of the challenge to climb a 'Munro' — a mountain more than 3,000 feet above sea level.

Sometimes we would abscond to the West of Ireland, where we were enchanted by its misty mountains and shimmering lakes, to say nothing of the music, humour and warm hospitality of its people. We always packed our small igloo tent, so that if the weather and scenery conspired to make it sufficiently enticing, we would spend a night under canvas close to nature — sometimes waking to an awe-inspiring sunrise, and sometimes to grey mist and drizzle.

On one magical occasion we pitched camp in a remote cove on the Isle of Mull, much to the bemusement of the elderly crofter and his wife who, solicitous for our well-being, but also curious about our strange predilection for austerity, paid us several visits during the course of the evening as we sat by our camp fire under the stars.

In the morning, sunrise set the sea ablaze and we sat spellbound by the edge of the rocky shore absorbing the splendour that was ours, uninterrupted and free of charge.

Then, the greatest thrill of all — a sea otter appeared. With a fish as big as himself, newly caught and held firmly in his claws, he nuzzled into a rock with his catch. After a minute or two he took to the water again and I thought that he had gone, but as an encore, he re-appeared with another silvery creature, and then, as if to let us know, that it was no fluke, he did it once more before disappearing for good. This flush of excitement lasted some 15 to 20 minutes, during which time I also took my breakfast on a rock at a distance of only 20 yards from our amphibious friend.

There were several other occasions when we preferred our tent to the comforts of bed and breakfast. We camped in the fields of Athenry — a meadow offered to us by a friendly farmer when we visited the charming town, coincidentally, on the occasion of its annual festival. And again on Achill Island when after an unforgettable jovial evening in a pub with three American nuns, dressed in mufti, we pitched on a cliff top, and paid the price for our impetuosity next morning when we awoke to rain and high winds.

Camping in the fields of Athenry

But there were other times too when I took off with friends. I well remember the hot July day in 1987 when we had just conquered another summit somewhere in the Yorkshire dales, and were relaxing on a carpet of level turf and taking in the glorious panorama, when we noticed a solitary figure labouring up the steep ascent from the opposite direction.

At a distance, we perceived a tall, slim, athletic young man making steady progress, but as he drew near, we saw that he was elderly — seventy if he was a day — but with a determined stride, a back like a ramrod, and a twinkling eye which revealed

a pleasant personality. He greeted us warmly,

'Hello, are you on the Coast to Coast?.... Me too.... This is my second day.... hoping to do it in ten. What about you, when did you start?'

'Five years ago.'

'What,.... you mean that?....There's a book in it .... yes, definitely a book in that.'

And off he strode, chuckling as he went, while we - *'the last of the summer wine'* - basked for a little longer under a cloudless summer sky.

Tony Redmond, Jim McCauley, Austin Hughes,

Harry Wallace, Harry Pepp and I were following Wainwright's famous Coast to Coast route from St. Bees in Cumbria to Robin Hood's Bay in Yorkshire — a ten-day walk, but in our case two days each July for five successive years. The physical challenge, the splendour of England's most beautiful countryside and comradeship kept us going over Lakeland fells and Yorkshire dales, but it must be said that, bed and breakfasting in stone-built inns with beamed ceilings, flagstone floors, good food and, most importantly, laughter nourished and quickened by fine hand-pumped ales made up the motivation that inspired an enthusiastic return each year, for it was very much a lads' affair.

It was at a hostelry in Kirkby Stephen, when gorged with a wholesome bar meal and about to embark on a jovial evening, that a telephone call to Gill produced a significant contribution to the evening's entertainment:

'Thank goodness you've called. What's a Knight of St. Gregory?'

'It's er.... how many letters?'

'No, it's not a crossword clue. I want to know what it's for.'

'What's what for?'

'What's a Knight of St. Gregory for?'

'Why do you want to know that? .... It's an award.... I suppose people get it for doing something special .... distinguished service to the Church. It's a Papal award. Anyway, what's it all about?'

'You're one.'

'One what?'

'One of them. Bishop Hitchen rang me at work today. He's been trying to contact you to tell you that the Pope has made you a Knight of St. Gregory.'

'Bloody hell!'

I then exploded with laughter that could be heard all over the pub and turned every head in my direction. Gill continued,

'Everybody here seems most impressed. What are you laughing at?'

'I dunno.... it's crazy.... Oh hell, I'd better not tell the lads.'

But it was obvious that there was something up, and they were oozing curiosity. There was no escape.

'What the hell was that all about?'

'You'll never believe it — not in a thousand years.'

'Premium bond up? ....Pools win?.... Gill's pregnant?'

'No, no and no!'

'Come on then. Don't keep us in suspense.'

'I've been made a Knight of St. Gregory.'

'You've what? .... What the hell for? .... You are joking?'

'God knows, but it's true. Hitch rang Gill this morning. It's going to be in the papers tomorrow.'

For a few seconds there was a stunned silence and then:

'Vin you've been ennobled and you haven't even got a horse.... or a sword!'

'I don't know about ennobled. I've been nobbled!'

There followed a feast of teasing and leg-pulling and all I could do was take it and outwardly beam while inwardly I puzzled over the astonishing news that had come like a bolt from the blue.

'Arise Sir Vin and get the beers in.'

Derek

'The joys and the hopes, the griefs and the anxieties
Of the men of this age, especially those who are poor
Or in any way afflicted, these too are the hopes, the
griefs and anxieties of the followers of Christ.'
(Vatican 2 Church in The Modern World)

He greeted me with a handshake but not a flicker of a smile:

'What kind of attendance are you expecting?'

'It's difficult to say. We have mailed all the parish groups and hopefully....'

'I didn't ask what you hoped for, I asked how many do you expect?'

It was clear that he was not in a good fettle. Perhaps something had upset him — or was he always like this? Without a moment's thought, I plucked a figure out of the air:

'Two hundred.'

Not so much as a grunt in reply as we walked up the aisle with rows of empty chairs on either side. I glanced at my watch — ten minutes to go.

'We'd better start on time,' I thought, 'or he might explode.'

St. Katherine's College, Liverpool, was the venue where I had been standing rather nervously at the entrance waiting to greet the Archbishop when he arrived. It was the 1979 Annual Assembly of the Archdiocesan Justice and Peace groups, and since I was the Chairperson of the Archdiocesan Justice and Peace Commission, it was appropriate that I should be there to welcome him on his arrival.

Because of his tetchy mood, I off-loaded him to

Derek and David at the launch of their book, 'Better Together'
Photo: Tom Murphy (Catholic Pictorial)

Cathy Piper of The Catholic Institute for International Relations and slipped away for a minute or two to urge people to occupy the front seats. I threw a glance out of the window and was relieved to see that the car park was starting to fill-up and within minutes so too was the hall.

The meeting went well. Derek, as we all called him, though never within earshot, gave an inspirational and seemingly off the cuff address, and Cathy Piper, speaking on Human Rights in Guatemala, was good value too. The follow-up discussion was lively, and I felt that I also had been in good form as chairperson. Though small talk was not Derek's strong point, nevertheless, after the meeting, there was a notable thaw in our

rapport, and I felt that I had survived my first encounter with the Archbishop reasonably well. Two days later, my wife and I received an invitation to a reception hosted by the Bishops of England and Wales in Archbishop's House Westminster, as part of their Low Week Conference.

Derek Worlock was Bishop of Portsmouth in 1973 when I moved from Northumberland to Liverpool to take up the headship of St. Edmund's Junior School in Waterloo. In 1975 with the deaths of Cardinal Heenan and Archbishop Beck, Westminster and Liverpool were vacant. Derek Worlock was widely tipped for the Cardinal's hat at Westminster, but I was hoping, because of his left-of-centre political stance, that he would come north. He did — arriving shortly after David Sheppard's appointment as Church of England Bishop of Liverpool, and there followed a deep friendship and one of the closest associations between the Catholic and Anglican Churches ever to take place in this country.

My own relationship with Derek also developed, though by no means at the same pace or to the same degree, and it was some years before I could enjoy anything that might resemble a relaxed and friendly conversation, for his personality required him to keep a role distance. Fraternal informality might easily produce a brusque response, and yet underneath he cherished friendship. His way of communicating affection or making known that you were valued was often by some grand gesture.

That he supported all my work for CAFOD was obvious and explicit, but his affirmation at a deeper level came when he conferred on me a Papal Knighthood.

In October 1991, he asked me to be his representative on a T.U.C. fact-finding delegation to Israel, taking in Jerusalem, the West Bank and the Gaza Strip, where I spoke to journalists, lawyers, doctors, trade unionists and clergy. I was welcomed by and enjoyed the warm hospitality of the Mayor of Bethlehem, a devout Catholic. Everything we saw then confirmed the reports of international lawyers who concluded that Israeli policies contravened the Geneva Convention on the treatment of people under occupation.

We witnessed widespread poverty and oppression among the Palestinians. Human rights abuses were widespread in the form of evictions to make way for Israeli settlers; schools and universities were closed for long periods of time to Palestinians, and journalists were beaten, imprisoned and their offices ransacked. This in turn produced a response from the oppressed. 'Intifada' was the term given to Palestinian resistance, which took the form of stone-throwing at soldiers, boycotts, strikes and graffiti. The military often responded with brutality, and in the Mosadek Hospital we saw many seriously injured children.

However, not all was gloom and despair. There was a glimmer of hope, for the Peace Now Movement, led by Dr. Mordchai Bar-On, an Israeli former soldier and politician, could muster 10,000 activists for a demonstration. But that was the only germ of good news that I had to take to my Archbishop and, while passing through Tel Aviv airport, my colleagues and I were assigned to separate rooms where we were grilled by Israeli Security, because we were known to have been hosted by Palestinian Arabs.

On my return I submitted a full written report to Archbishop Worlock along with two personal messages, one from Canon Naim Ateek of St. George's Anglican Cathedral in Jerusalem pleading for the Churches to make representations to our Government on behalf of the oppressed Palestinian people. The other was from the Mayor of Bethlehem asking the Church in England to forge links of solidarity with the Christian minority - *'a precious commodity,'* he stressed, *'which is in danger of becoming extinct.'*

Back home, I was invited to Archbishop's House, where for two hours I enjoyed warm hospitality, friendly, informal conversation and talked through my report, a copy of which he said he would take to Rome. It was obvious that he was fully conversant with the state of affairs in Israel, and as always, he showed deep concern not only for the suffering poor but also for those who worked for peace and justice in that troubled country.

Derek by now had become much more to me than my Archbishop. He was my friend and I loved him, but I still addressed him, 'Your Grace'. I had enjoyed many happy occasions with him in his home in Green Lane. Sometimes these were small gatherings such as birthday celebrations. When I hosted overseas visitors, a frequent occurrence,

A delegation from Asia is hosted by the Archbishop

milestones in his priestly life, namely the fortieth anniversary of his ordination as a priest and his twenty-fifth as bishop. But the private and intimate, one-to-one conversations that I shared with him were the most precious — especially when he occasionally confided in me some of his joys and disappointments.

But by far the most moving occasion was in 1995, when he was the official starter at the CAFOD Christmas Run. Every year I had invited him, and every year he very graciously declined:

'I must give way to one of my younger episcopal colleagues.'

he always invited me to bring them to Archbishop's House for hospitality and an informal chat about the problems in their respective countries. He would compare and contrast their situation with that in our own country, and invariably never forget to mention the important part he had played at significant moments in the life of the Church, for as Clifford Longley observed in his work, *The Worlock Archive,* 'He was never a man to let modesty deny him his rightful place in history'. There were also the grand occasions when he celebrated the

But Christmas that year was different, for he was dying. Therefore, I did not include my usual invitation with my Christmas card.... and then I heard that he was coming anyway. I could hardly believe it and I knew that he was doing it for me. The day before the Run he was made a Companion of Honour in The Queen's New Year's Honours List. Could I ever forget his sacrifice? Unable to walk unaided, he was driven to the college entrance by his ever faithful and trusted chaplain, Father John Furnival, from where he was transported in a wheelchair to the Director's room where Monsignor John Devine sat him at an open window overlooking the start of the Run. Standing on the platform, I announced to one thousand runners and their many supporters,

'Ladies and gentlemen, Her Majesty The Queen yesterday appointed Archbishop Worlock Companion Of Honour. Today, he is our official starter, so let us turn to the window where he is greeting us and give him three rousing cheers, hip, hip....'

I then took the microphone to his window where a very frail figure in clerical garb and pectoral cross waved feebly. We could hardly hear his weak and gentle tones:

'On your marks....get set....'

At the crack of the pistol, I joined the stampede as usual, but before doing so, I gave a final wave to Derek, who returned it with a faint smile and I took off, carrying with me a jumble of emotions, knowing that he would not be with us for much longer, and also that this was the last time I would participate in the CAFOD Christmas Run.

A few weeks later, I was to undertake one of my last duties for CAFOD — to lead a small delegation to Sri Lanka for three weeks. By now, and for various reasons, I had little stomach for the task. Before leaving I went to see Derek, who was now confined to his bed. Father John showed me to his room and then left us alone for a full half-hour. I was conscious of the privilege it was for me to be sitting by the death-bed of my Archbishop — but not just because he was an Archbishop — more so because he had given prophetic witness on the great issues of his day. He had for example stood alone among his fellow bishops in declaring himself to be a unilateralist during the great debate concerning nuclear weapons, and had taken an option for the poor — not only in Latin America where some of his priests worked in the shanties but also in his own inner city and council estates, where his people were the poor and oppressed on his doorstep. He was their champion. But I was also immensely conscious of the privilege it was to be sitting at the bedside, as a friend, of one who could also count Popes, Presidents and Prime Ministers among his friends, for he had rubbed shoulders with the great and good of his day.

Archbishop Derek with Vin

For a moment I reflected, however, that I was now also in the presence of someone as powerless as the poor he had loved and served so well. It was all over and he knew it. There was a peace and tranquillity in his whole demeanour.

Pale, thin and feeble, his voice weak and breaking, role distance was no longer an issue and with arms outstretched, he welcomed me warmly as a friend.

> 'Hello, Father, I'm going away again for a few weeks to Sri Lanka, and I thought that I should come and see you before I go.'

> 'How appropriate …… I am so glad that you have come…… In recent years, we have shared so much, now we can share a little of what's left. Take my hand and say a prayer.'

Spontaneous prayer does not come easy to me unless I'm alone, so I was taken somewhat aback when my Archbishop asked me to pray with him.

As it happened it did not turn out to be an embarrassment so much as a deeply emotional experience. I took his hand as he asked me to and I spoke to the Lord, then I spoke to Derek and then again to the Lord.... and repeated it again and again.... and then I said, *'Goodbye, Father.'* He replied, *'Have a good trip'*.

When I returned from Sri Lanka he had gone to heaven.

Not Yet....

'The secret of happiness is to fall in love with what you have to do for a living.' — *George Burns on his 94th birthday*

Cardinal Heenan entitled his autobiography, 'Not The Whole Truth'. I might have given mine the title, 'Not The Whole Story'.

But enough is enough — except perhaps to pay tribute to those in my life who are very special, for I am blessed with a happy family life.

It is, therefore, most fitting that I should conclude with a word of thanks to my wife, who has put up with so many of my idiosyncrasies over the years and, more recently, endured my absences while I was on CAFOD business — not to mention my landing her with a steady stream of overseas visitors, and never a word of complaint. *'What never?'... 'Well, hardly ever!'*

Our greatest blessing is a united and happy family. With spouses, and seven grandchildren at the last count, we make quite a tribe, and turn a few heads when we come together to celebrate summer holidays — usually in the Highlands of Scotland or the West of Ireland.

Some years ago while walking on the Isle of Islay in the Hebrides, we stopped to take some refreshment in the fishing village of Portnahaven and, sitting on a bench outside the pub, we got talking to an old salt. After a few pleasantries I ventured to ask,

'Have you lived here all your life?'

'Not yet,' he replied.

And so, this, the last and very briefest of chapters, is hopefully not the last chapter of my life....not yet. But you never know!

Therefore I shall not tempt fate — not a word about aspirations, hopes and dreams, for as someone once said,

'If you want to give God a good laugh tell Him about your plans for the future.'

In the twilight of life,
God will not judge us
On our earthly possessions
And human success,
But rather on how much
We have loved.'
St. John of the Cross